DATA SCIENCE FROM SCRATCH

*Comprehensive Beginners Guide
To Learn Data Science From Scratch*

HENRY GEORGE

Table of Contents

Introduction

"A data scientist is a professional who outshines any software engineer in statistics and outshines any statistician in software engineering."

\- Josh Wills.

In the past decade, there has been an increase in the demand for data scientists in the IT and business world. This is due to the fact that a lot of companies were gathering data on their clients and they needed experts to analyze them. A data scientist is a person who combines statistics, programming, and research skills to extract and interpret information from large amounts of data. Most data scientists started their careers as a data analyst or statistician and further expanded their roles to include programming.

The thousand-mile journey to become a data scientist begins with reading and following the instructions in this book. It is designed to transform beginners and people who are yet to develop a program, into top-notch programmers. It will also teach the basic concepts of statistics, probability, and machine learning that will help you get started in your career as a data scientist.

An efficient data scientist is a problem-solver and a strategist who uses well-structured algorithms to provide solutions. Do you have the desire to carry out fascinating projects and solve real-life problems? Then this book is for you. Let's get started, shall we?

Part 1

This book is divided into two parts, introduction to Python programming and the application Python in statistic, probability, machine learning. Part 1 starts teaching Python at the rudimentary level and instills the reader with enough skill to be able to write advanced programs in data science.

Chapter 1

Introduction to Data and Programming

The world is overflowing with data. Most websites are designed to track every click the user makes. Smartphones are getting better and faster at tracking your location. Some watches do more than just tell time. They record what you eat, the steps you take, the way you sleep, and even the number of times your heart beats in a minute. As of May 2019, about 4 billion people gained access to the Internet and input various types of data. Somewhere in these data are the solutions to various problems. As a data scientist, you have to seek means to find them.

Data science is a combination of programming, statistics, and research skills. This book will cover all three skills. The first thing you need to do is to learn how to run a program, and when the time is right, the mathematical aspects of data science will come into play. The instructions will be in the form of examples to maximize understanding. Python is the programming language taught in this book.

Why Python?

There are a lot of arguments about the first language to master when starting data science. A few people suggested R, some mentioned Java, but the majority supported Python. Python has been called "a great introductory language," it's an object-oriented, high-level programming language. Guido van Rossum created the language, and it was adopted in 1989. He named the program after his favorite comedy show, Monty Python. He got the idea from the ABC language he had assisted in creating.

Python can be used to develop online and offline games, create graphic user interfaces, network programming, data analysis, scripting, machine learning, artificial intelligence, and many more. As an Object-oriented language, the objects and data structures used in creating a program are subject to manipulation by the user.

Writing codes in Python is very similar to writing instructions in English. Therefore, Python as a language is not machine-readable and requires an interpreter to translate it into a machine-readable language. The codes can only run after translation.

Some programming languages become obsolete after a few years of operation and are substituted with languages that are more effective and relevant. Python is still relevant and very much useful despite being 30 years old. That's why it is very popular among people who are learning how to program for the first time. It was chosen as an introductory language for the following reasons:

- It's much easier to comprehend than any other high-level programming language.
- You don't have to pay for it. It's free.
- It's reasonably flexible and allows for easy experimentation.
- You will gain access to a lot of data science libraries, which will be useful to you in the long run.
- Its built-in properties are well constructed.
- It's much easier to learn other programming languages when you learn Python first.

Having a good knowledge of Python is fundamental to becoming a successful software developer.

How to Install Python?

You can download Python from the website. The most recent version of Python is the 3.7.4 upgrade released in July 2019. However, the best version to download for data science is the 2.7.16 upgrade released in March 2019. Some important libraries necessary for data scientists are only compatible with the 2.7 version. After downloading, click on the .exe file to install it.

You also need to download pips, which is a package installer for Python. It will help you install the necessary 3rd-party packages. You can download it from the website.

NB: You also need to download pip to install most of the libraries needed for data science.

Your First Launch

Restart your system after installation for the application to run smoothly after launching. Launch your app. Now it's time to explore the features of the application. There are two options available, the Integrated Development and Learning Environment (IDLE) and the command line window. You can access them through the shortcuts in the program file. The major difference between both windows is that you can copy, edit, and cut previous programs in IDLE.

You can also work in script mode in IDLE, this allows you to write programs that won't run immediately. Click the *New file option* on the file toolbar to get into script mode. When you're ready, you can run the program by clicking the run module option in the *Run* toolbar or you press F5.

How to Print Hello World!

A lot of programmers believe that printing "Hello World!" as your first command will bring good luck. Your first mission is to print "Hello World!"

1. Launch either the Command line or the IDLE window.
2. The ">>>" is called the command prompt. It's on the first editable line. Type after the prompt

    ```
    print("Hello World!")
    ```

3. Press enter to print.

    ```
    Mission successful. Hello World!
    ```

print ("Hello World!") is a statement. A statement is known as an executable command in programming languages. Note that the "p" in print is written in lowercase, commands are written in lowercase. The parentheses are very important, it will contain the text to be printed. The quotation marks are also very important, they define the words to be printed. By the time you're done with the book, you'll realize quotation marks and parentheses have a huge role to play in writing codes.

Print"Hello World!"   wrong.

print (Hello World!)   wrong.

print 'hello world'   is only accepted in Version 2.

NB: It's best to learn the method that accepted in all versions.

How to Display Python's Design Principles

Python has a list of principles built into the app. It's called the Zen of Python.

To display it, you can

1. Type "`import this`" after the command prompt >>>.

2. Press the 'enter' button to run.

You can find the words on the website. Mission successful if your command ran without a hitch.

From the words imported, it's quite clear that Python was created to be easy and readable.

How to Exit Python

Python can be closed in three ways.

1. Type exit()
2. Type quit()
3. Hold down control and Z, then press enter.

Chapter 2

Python 101

Python Syntax

The set of rules that specifies how the users and system write and interpret codes on Python is called Python syntax. Prior to writing and running programs on python, you have to get accustomed to its syntax.

Indentation

A lot of programming language separate blocks of code with curly braces, but not Python. Rather, it uses indentation to set the boundary of a block of code.

Before you can grasp the purpose of indentation in Python, you have to understand what a block of code means. A block of code is a group of statements executed one after the other. Do you remember what a statement is? It's an executable command.

```
if opinion == yes:  ------------------------i
        print("I love Python")-------------ii
        loop = True       ----------------iii
```

Line iii, and iii make up "if" block of code. The system runs line i, then line ii, and finally line iii. There is an indentation in line ii in the example above. You indent by pressing tab on the next line. While you can also use space to indent (4 spaces are equivalent to a tab), never use both space and tab at the same time. The level of indentation matters, statements within the same level of indentation make up a block.

It's possible to have more than one set of indentation, there's no limit. For example

```
>>> def house_rent_cost(weeks):
    cost=35*weeks
    if weeks >= 8
                cost -= 70
                    elif weeks >= 3:
                cost -= 20
                    return cost
```

How many blocks are present in the code above?

NB:

- The IDLE window automatically indents your code.
- If you don't indent, Python will automatically interpret your statements as separate.
- If there's an error interpreting one of the statements, the entire program won't run.

It's quite common for programmers to indent in other languages (to make their codes neat and readable); Python just makes it necessary.

Comments

Comments refer to statements added to a code that describes or explains what it does. Leaving a comment can help you and other person reviewing your code understand the purpose of your code. A comment has no impact on the code, as the Python interpreter automatically skips it. You can create a comment at any point in the code by starting the comment with the hash symbol '#'. The moment the interpreter recognizes the hash symbol, it skips the words until it reaches the end of the line.

To write comments that span across multiple lines, you can either start each line with the hash symbol or you can surround the comments with triple quotes """" """".

```
def increase_income(rating,sal,percentage):
        #increase income of workers
        """increase rating based on rating and
                percentage
rating 1- 6 10% increase"""
```

The two methods of starting comments were used. A major advantage is that it enhances your code, makes it readable.

Variables

A variable can easily be defined as a placeholder. A variable is used to direct the computer to save a value that is needed later in the program, the programmer just needs to type the name of the variable to access and modify it. You can think of a variable as a box that stores a value, which you can access at any point in time.

The holding ability of a variable is more flexible in Python than any other programming language. Python variables can hold both letters and integers, while the other languages can only hold one type at a time, either letters or integers, not both in the same variable. Basically, a variable can be assigned "10a". This isn't possible in any other programming language. Once an integer, always an integer.

The Naming of Variables

The name of a variable is called an identifier. An identifier is a name given to a function, variable, constant, class, etc.

Naming a variable is quite easy, but the naming is guided by a set of rules. They are:

- The variable can only be named with a number, variable, and an underscore. The name of the variable cannot begin with a number, using a letter or underscore is permitted. The use of spaces in a variable name is not allowed, rather you can use an underscore to replace the space where necessary. For example, `number 1 is wrong, number_1 is right`.

- Do not use a Python keyword as the name of a variable. You will find out more about Python keywords later in this chapter.

- When naming the variable, select a name that is relevant to the information stored in the variable. This will allow you to recall the name of the variable easily. For example, if you want a variable to store the number of bags in a store, it's much easier to remember the name if you named it `bag_number rather than numberb`.

- The name of a variable should not be excessively long. It's preferable if the name describes the information stored in 2 words, a maximum of three words. For example, `bag_number` is better than `number_of_bags_in_store`.

- Human errors can occur when using small letter l and capital letter O, as it can be mistaken as 1 and 0 respectively. Take care when using both letters. For example, when naming a variable to store the number of lengths, it's better to name it `number_length` rather than `number_l` as the latter may be read as number 1.

The rules above also guide the naming of every other type of identifier.

Storing a Value in a Variable

A variable can only be stored when it is assigned a value. To assign a value to a variable, you have to use the equals to symbol "=".

Examples.

1. If there are twelve bags in a store, how will you store it as a variable?

   Solution: After the prompt, type "bag_number = 12."

   ```
   >>> bag_number = 12
   ```

   If that is the command you wrote, you have successfully assigned **bag_number** a value. To verify this type "print(bag_number)" after the command prompt, 12 will appear on the following line.

   ```
   >>>print(bag_number)
   12
   ```

   N.B: Quotation marks are not used within the parentheses because **bag_number** is a variable. It's already defined. But if it's just a statement, it needs to be defined with quotation marks to print.

2. How will you modify the values of the variable?

Solution: There are two ways to change the value of a variable. You can either assign the variable another value or you can perform a calculation to get your desired value.

3. If 8 bags were sold, how will you change the value of `bag_number` to 4?

Solution: After the prompt, type

Option 1-   `bag_number = 4`

Option 2-   `bag_number = bag_number - 8`

Option 3-   `bag_number = bag_number/3`

Verify your modification with `print(bag_number)`. 4 should appear on the next line.

4. How do you assign the value of a variable to another variable?

Solution: Simply assign the variables to each other. To assign the value of `bag_number` to `number_store`, type

```
bag_number = number_store
```

NB: `number_store` must be an existing variable to prevent errors.

Chapter 3

Python Data Types

Python offers several data types to satisfy the requirements of users and developers for workable data. The data types that will be discussed in this chapter include:

- Numbers (Numeric data type),
- String,
- List,
- Set,
- Dictionary, and
- Date and time.

Numbers (Numeric Data Type)

Originally, there were four built-in numeric data types in Python, but in Version 3, two of the data types were combined into one. The numeric data types are:

1. Integer
2. Float Numbers
3. Complex Numbers
4. Long (it's now part of Integer)

A major advantage of using Python is that when you run your program, it automatically recognizes the numeric data type even if you don't declare it's type.

1. Integers

They are whole numbers that do not contain a decimal point. It can be a positive or a negative number, as long as it does not have a decimal point or number. There are four main types of integers:

— *Regular integers:* These are just regulars numbers e.g 496, -324, 17, etc.
— *Octal literals:* These are numbers written to base 8. To declare this type of integer, you have to begin the numbers with 0O or 0o (zero and lower case o or upper case O, in that order).
Example

```
>>> b = 0o24567 # each number must be less than 8
>>> print b
    10615   # the interpreter converted b to its natural (base 10)
```

— *Hexadecimal literals:* These are numbers written to base 16. To declare this type of integer, you have to begin the numbers with 0X or 0x (zero and lower case x or upper case X, in that order).
Example

```
>>> z = 0x24567
>>> print z
    148839  # the interpreter converted z to its natural (base 10)
>>> y = 0XABCD
>>> print y
43981
```

— *Binary literals*: These are numbers written to base 2. To declare this type of integer, you have to begin the numbers with 0B or 0b (zero and lower case b or upper case B, in that order).

Example

```
>>> x = 0B011011
>>> print x
# the interpreter converted x to its natural
(base 10)
```

2. Floating Numbers

These are real numbers with decimal points. They are popularly referred to as floats. They can also be written in the form where e represents the 10th power.

NB: All integers are floats but not all floats are integers.

```
>>> 5.4e3
5400.0
>>>5.4e2
540
```

1. Complex Numbers

These are numbers that contain both real and imaginary numbers. E.g

```
>>> z = 4 + 5j     # 4 and 5 are real numbers
>>> y = 7 + 2j     # j is an imaginary number
>>> w = 3 +6j
>>> u = z + y + w
>>> print u
(14+13j)
```

Strings

Strings are groups of letters and/or characters delimited with quotation marks, single or double. Once a string is declared, it can't be changed.

How to Assign a String

To assign a string to a variable, you have to define it with quotation marks ' ' or " " or " " " " " " . Triple quotations marks are used for strings that spill over to another line.

Examples

1. How will you assign the string 'blue' to a variable (bag_colour)?

```
Typing         bag_colour = blue          is very
wrong.
```

Solution: Type

```
>>>bag_colour = 'blue'
```

To verify the assignment print bag_number. The output should be

```
>>>print (bag_colour)
```

```
    blue
```

2. Assign a multi-line string.

Solution:

```
>>> multi_line = ''' The road to becoming a
fully qualified data scientist is long, but with
```

```
discipline and the right mindset, you can make
it shorter.
 There are no shortcuts to data science, but
there are ways to shorten the journey, reading
this book is one of them. '''
>>>print (multi_line)
The road to becoming a fully qualified data
scientist is long, but with discipline and the
right mindset, you can make it shorter.
There are no shortcuts to data science, but
there are ways to shorten the journey, reading
this book is one of them.
```

NB:

- You have to use matching quotation marks, do not start with a single quotation mark and end with a double quotation mark.

- To print a quotation mark within a string, you have to insert a backslash '\'.

```
>>>statement1 = ' I love Python, it\'s very
cool. '
>>>print ( statement1 )
I love Python, it's very cool.
```

Concatenation, Repetition, and Slicing of Strings

Concatenation is the process of joining two strings together. Repetition is the process of repeating a string for a specified number of times while slicing is the method used to extract certain parts of a string.

Examples

```
>>> line1 = " I just love writing programs with
Python. "
>>> line2 = " It's very powerful and easy to
understand. "
>>> line3 = ' It also doesn\'t take much time to
learn. '
>>> print ( line1 + line2 + line3)#concatenation
I just love writing programs with Python. It's
very powerful and easy to understand. It also
doesn't take much time to learn.   #output

>>> print ( line2*4 )                #repitition
It's very powerful and easy to understand. It's
very powerful and easy to understand. It's very
powerful and easy to understand.      It's very
powerful and easy to understand.    #output
```

In Python, the index of data types starts from 0. To perform splicing, you have to know how the Python interpreter counts a string.

```
>>> string1 = ' Hello World!'
>>> print ( string1[4:10])
>>> print ( string1 [1:5])
```

The index of string1 =

-12	-11	-10	-9	-8	-7	-6	-5	-4	-3	-2	-1
H	E	l	l	o		W	O	r	l	d	!
0	1	2	3	4	5	6	7	8	9	10	11

The ouput:

```
>>> print ( string1[4:10])
o Worl
>>> print ( string1 [1:5])
ello
```

lower() and upper() function

lower() and upper() functions are used to convert the letters in a string to lower and upper case respectively.

Examples

```
>>> string1 = 'Hello World!'
>>> string2 = 'hello world!'
>>> print ( string1.lower())
hello world!
>>> print ( string2.upper())
HELLO WORLD!
```

Chapter 4

In-built Python Features

Python Keywords

Python keywords are words that have a specific function in programming. The words cannot be used to name a variable, define a function, constant or any other type of identifier. Using a keyword for a purpose different from its function will lead to problems when running your program. The keywords are listed in alphabetical order:

```
and         as          assert
break       class       continue
def         del         elif
else        except      false
finally     for         from
global      if          import
in          is          lambda
non local   not         or
pass        print       raise
return      true        try
while       with        yield
```

You already encountered some of the keywords above in the previous topics. Uou will keep seeing and learning about them because every single one of them has an important and specific use.

With diligence and constant practice, you will know and be able to use each and every keyword ad-lib.

Functions

A function is an organized block of code that is used to execute a specific command. Using a function makes coding easy because once it is defined, you can use it to perform an action at any point in the program. You have two options when it comes to functions, you can either use Python's built-in function or you can create your own. The built-in functions will be discussed later. Your mission right now is to learn how to create your own function.

How to Define a Function

Syntax:

```
def name_of_function( parameters ):
#docstring
    statements
    return [ Expression ]
```

The Python keyword '*def*' begins with the function block. It is immediately followed by the name of the function and parentheses '()'. The parameter(s) expected is placed within the parentheses. The first line of every function code block must end with a colon ':'. The docstring comment is customarily used to explain what the function does. It's good to document the purpose of the function as it's difficult and laborious to memorize the purpose of every function you create and the purpose of the functions built-in. The statements contain the operation the function will perform. The 'return' keyword exits the function code block and prints the value of the expression. If the return statement doesn't have an expression, it will exit the code block.

NB: The naming of a function follows the same rules that guide the naming of a variable.

Examples

1. To create a new function that multiplies two numbers:

```
>>> def multiply( c, d ):
        product = c * d
        return product
```

2. To create a function that prints a statement:

```
>>> def print_function( sentence ):
        print "Hi : ", sentence
        return
```

How to Call a Function

To call a function, you have to write the name of the function and fill its parentheses with the necessary parameters.

Examples

1. To use the multiply function:

```
>>>   multiply ( 3, 5 )
              5
```

2. To use the print_function:

```
>>>print_function( 'This    is    a    function    that
prints    the    sentence    written    within    the
parenthesis.' )
```

Hi :   This is a function that prints the
sentence written within the parenthesis.

Built-in Python Functions

There are 68 built-in python functions. Python is much more
powerful with the functions, it's faster and easier to code. The built-
in functions are listed below in an alphabetical order:

abs()	all()	any()
ascii()	bin()	bool()
bytearray()	bytes()	callable()
chr()	classmethod()	compile()
complex()	delattr()	dict()
dir()	divmod()	enumerate()
eval()	exec()	filter()
float()	format()	frozenset()
getattr()	globals()	hasattr()
hash()	help()	hex()
id()	__import__()	input()
int()	isinstance()	issubclass()
iter()	len( )	list()
locals()	map()	max()
memoryview()	min()	next()
object()	oct( )	open()
ord()	pow( )	print()
property()	range( )	repr()
reversed()	round( )	set()
setattr()	slice()	sorted()
staticmethod()	str()	sum()
super()	tuple()	type()
vars()	zip()	

You may never need to use some of the functions in your entire
career as a data scientist. However, knowing how to use some of the

functions is important. You already know how to use of some functions (such as hex(), bin(), and oct ()), the other functions that you need for a career in data science are explained in this chapter.

The print() Function

You learned about the print() function in Chapter 1, this will serve as a little reminder. The function is used to print different types of statements, values, and expressions. Aside from parentheses and quotation marks, commas are also important when printing. To print multiple variables within a print() function, you have to separate them with a comma.

Example

1. If x = "sister", y = "boy", and z = 15, how will you print them using one

    ```
    print() function?
    ```

Solution:

    ```
    >>> print(x,y,z)
        sister boy 15
    ```

Blank space will be displayed between the variables.

The input() Function

Some programs are designed to get input from sources external to the Python window, examples of such external sources include: the internet, database, keyboard, storage location on another computer, mouse clicks, etc. Since the most common source of input is the keyboard, Python created the input() function to allow users to gather input from the keyboard.

When Python's interpreter encounters an input function, the flow of the program stops until the user enters an input. The user's input is interpreted and converted to a string by the input() function.

Python also created an optional parameter for the input() function, it's called the prompt string. It holds text that prompts the user to enter the necessary information. Here is an example of how the input() function and the prompt string works:

This program asks for the name, age and educational background of the user

```python
full_name = input("Hi, can you enter your full name? ")
print("Wow, your name sounds intelligent" + full_name + "!")
age = input("How old were you on your last birthday? ")
print("So, you are already Really, you are " + age + " years old, " + name + "!")
level = input("What is your highest level of education? ")
print(+ level + ", well done! ")
```

NB: When writing text in the print() function, you have to be careful with spacing. You have to leave spaces at the appropriate place so your text won't get muddled up. Visualize how you want your statement to look like and write your code around that.

When you run the code written above, it will bring up something like this

```
Hi, can you enter your full name?
```

The text above is a prompt asking the user to enter the necessary information. Press enter, after inputting the necessary information.

```
Luke Evans
Wow, your name sounds intelligent Luke Evans!
How old were you on your last birthday?
```

As you can see the spaces used in the code are appropriate and the name entered was able to fit in well.

```
19
Really, you are 19 years old, Luke Evans!
```

Can you see how interactive the program is? It's engaging the user while asking for information.

```
What     is     your     highest     level     of     education?
University
University, well done!
```

You can use the input function to request different types of information. As a data scientist, you can create a program that will gather data from a specific group of people. The program below filters the type of people answering the questions by placing an 'if' condition on the answer given.

```
full_name = input("Hi, can you enter your full
name? ")
print ("Wow, your name sounds intelligent " +
full_name + "!")
age = input("How old were you on your last
birthday? ")
print("Really, you are " + age + " years old, "
+ name + "!")
if age == '18':
```

```python
        print("Excellent, this questionnaire is for
you!")
    else:
        print("Thank you for filling the survey.")
        quit()
```

At this point, if the answer of the user isn't 18, the program will end. quit() will close the program. But, if the answer is 18, the program goes on.

```python
level = input("What is your highest level of
education? ")
sport = input("Are you engaged in any form of
sporting activities in your " +level + "?")
if sport == 'yes':
    print("Awesome!")
    sport_type = input("What type of sport? ")
else:
    print("Thank you for filling the survey.")
    quit()
```

The program is constructed to only keep running if the input entered by the user matches the requirements of the programmer. The next step for a data scientist is to analyze and process the data gotten from the survey. Chapter 3 will speak more on how to acquire and process data.

NB: How to use the 'if' and 'else' statement will also be explained later.

max()

This function is used to print the highest value among a set of values or variables.

Example

1. 15 students took a test and got the following scores:

12, 75, 87, 34, 45, 56, 67, 78, 87, 98, 54, 34, 65, 87, 42.

Print the highest score.

Solution:

```
>>> max(12, 75, 87, 34, 45, 56, 67, 78, 87, 98,
54, 34, 65, 87, 42)
   98
```

2. There are five brands of bags in a store: Gucci, Chanel, Louis Vuitton, Michael Kors, and Buscemi.

Gucci = 17 bags

Chanel =56 bags

Louis Vuitton =54 bags

Michael Kors = 34 bags

Buscemi = 23 bags. Pick out the largest number of bags among the brands.

Solution:

```
>>>    max(   gucci,    chanel,    louis_vuitton,
michael_kors, buscemi)
   56
```

min()

This function is used to print the lowest value among a set of values or variables.

Examples

1. 15 students took a test and got the following scores:

12, 75, 87, 34, 45, 56, 67, 78, 87, 98, 54, 34, 65, 87, 42.

Print the highest score.

Solution:

```
>>> min(12, 75, 87, 34, 45, 56, 67, 78, 87, 98,
54, 34, 65, 87, 42)
   12
```

2. There are five brands of bags in a store: Gucci, Chanel, louis Vuitton, Michael Kors, and Buscemi.

Gucci = 17 bags

Chanel =56 bags

Louis Vuitton =54 bags

Michael Kors = 34 bags

Buscemi = 23 bags. Pick out the lowest number of bags among the brands.

Solution:

```
>>>    min(   gucci,    chanel,    louis_vuitton,
michael_kors, buscemi)
   17
```

len()

The function prints the number of items inside a variable.

Example

1. Print the number of brands in the store.

```
>>>      bag_brands    =     'gucci',     'chanel',
'louis_vuitton', 'michael_kors', 'buscemi'
    print (len(bag_brands))
    5
```

2. Print the number of characters in a string.

```
>>>  bag_brands = 'Michael kors'
        print (len(bag_brands))       #this is used
to count in string slicing
   12
     >>>  print ( bag_brands[1:6] )
    ichae
```

range()

The range() function is used to produce a set of numbers. Range(n) will produce a set of numbers that starts from 0 and ends at n-1. For example, range(13) is equivalent to [0, 1, 2, 3, 4, 5, 6, 7, 8, 9, 10, 11, 12]. For range(2, 15), the numbers start at 2 and end at 14(15-1).

[2, 3, 4, 5, 6, 7, 8, 9, 10, 11, 12, 14]

range(2, 15, 3) means the numbers will start from 2, end at 14, and will move 3 numbers per step. It is equivalent to [2, 5, 8, 11, 14]

Syntax for range():

range(start, stop, size_of_step)

Chapter 5

Basic Operators

Python operators are symbols and words used to execute operations on values and variables. There are seven categories of operators used in Python:

1. Arithmetic Operators
2. Logical Operators
3. Relational Operators
4. Bitwise Operators
5. Membership Operators
6. Assignment Operators
7. Identity Operators.

For the purpose of this book, only 4 of the operators will be discussed.

Arithmetic Operators

These are operators that perform mathematical operations. You can use the operators to create algorithms that automatically solve mathematical problems. There are seven types of arithmetic operators:

Addition

This operator adds two or more values together. The same addition symbol '+' used for normal mathematical expressions is used for addition in Python.

Examples

1. How do you add 5 and 3 in Python?

Solution: type 5+3 after the prompt, then press enter

```
>>> 5+3
      8
```

2. How do you add variables i and j together?

Solution: The first thing you have to do is declare i and j, then you add then together.

```
>>>i = 15                    >>>i = 21
    j = 21                       j = 15
    i+j                          (i+j)
```

Both methods are correct. When you run it, 36 will display on the next line.

Subtraction

This operator subtracts one value from another. The symbol that represents subtraction in Python is '−'.

Example

1. How do you subtract 3 from 5 if i is 3 and j is 5?

```
        Solution:              >>>i = 3
                                   j = 5
                                   j-i
                                   2
```

Multiplication

This operator multiples two values. The symbol used for this operation is different from the symbol used for normal mathematical expressions. The asterisk '*' symbol is used for multiplication in Python.

Example

1. How do you multiply i and j in Python if i is 6 and j is 7?

```
Solution:>>> i = 6
            j = 7
            i*j
            42
```

Division.

This operator performs the division operation. The slash '/' symbol the carries out division operation in Python. Python 2.7 automatically performs floor division when '/' is used. To perform normal division operations, you have to import it by typing

```
>>> from _future_ import division
```

Example

1. How do you divide i by j if i is 15 and j is 5?

```
Solution: >>> i = 16
  j =5
  i/j
  3.2
```

Floor Division

This operator performs the division operation and produces a result without the decimal number(s). The symbol for this operator is double slash '//'.

Examples

1. How many 15's can you get from 100?
Solution:

```
>>> 100 // 15
6
```

2. How many times will i divide j if i 2 and j is 33?
Solution:

```
>>> i = 2
j = 33
j // i
16
```

Exponent

The exponent operator performs the 'raise to power' function in Python. The symbol used to perform an exponential calculation is '**'

Examples

1. If i is equal to 3, how do you get the value of i^2?

```
Solution: >>> i = 3
i**2 #i is raised to the power of 2
9
```

2. If j is equal to 5, how will you get the value of j^3?

```
Solution: >>> j = 5
          j**3     #j is raised to the power of 3
          125
```

Modulus

This operator produces the value leftover after performing a division operation. The percentage symbol is used for modulus in Python is '%'

Examples

1. What is the remainder when 50 is divided by 3?

```
Solution:
                    >>>50 % 3
                    2
```

2. What is leftover when 100 is divided by 17?

```
Solution:
                    >>> 100 % 17
                    15
```

Operator	Addition	Subtraction	Multiplication	Division	Floor division	Exponent	Modulus
Symbol	+	-	*	/	//	**	%

Arithmetic operators and their respective symbols.

Exercise 1: How to use basic arithmetic operators to perform operations on data extracted from a bar.

A couple celebrated their engagement party in a bar. They had 22 male and 28 female friends. The fiancé instructed the waiters to divide the guests into 3 groups, serve one group whiskey, the other group gin and tonic, and the last group beer. Each group had equal numbers of people. The guests who chose not to join a group got water. Before the drinks were served, each man had to pick a female partner to dance with. Not all women got to dance. At midnight the guests were given gift bags, the men got two bags while the women got three gift bags. Use the data given to solve the following questions.

   a. How many guests did the couple have?
   b. How many guests were in each group?
   c. How many guests got water?
   d. Calculate how many bags were given to the men, women, and the total number of bags?
   e. Square the number of male guests then divide it by the number of female guests.
   f. How many women didn't have a partner to dance with?

Solution.

Use script mode in IDLE to write the codes so they won't be interpreted immediately.

```
num_maleguest = 22
num_femaleguest = 28
total_guest = num_femaleguest + num_maleguest
                              #addition
```

```python
print (" a. There are " +str(total_guest) + "
guests in the bar")
num_pplgroup = total_guest//3
                                        #floor division
water_ppl = total_guest%3
                                        #modulus
print (" b. There are " +str(num_pplgroup) + "
people in a group.")
print (" c. " +str(water_ppl) + " people got
water.")
ttl_malebag = num_maleguest * 2
                                        #multiplication
ttl_femalebag = num_femaleguest * 3
ttl_giftbag = ttl_femalebag + ttl_malebag
print (" d.  Men were given" +str(ttl_malebag) + "
bags,  women were given " +str(ttl_femalebag) + "
bags, and " +str(ttl_giftbag)+ " bags were given in
total.")
square = (num_maleguest**2)/ num_femaleguest
                        #exponentiation, division
print (" e. The answer is "+str(square))
print ( "f. " +str(num_femaleguest -
num_maleguest)+ " women didn't get to dance.")
#subtraction
```

The question above tested your knowledge of variables, comments, and arithmetic operation. You even learned how to print a variable. Most codes will require knowledge and manipulation of various aspects of programming. Look for more questions to practice. The more you practice, the better you get at coding!

NB: The str() function is used to convert a non-string into a string. It is especially useful when you want to print the integer value of a variable in a sentence without the appearance of a comma. If the string is to be placed in between sentences, the plus symbol '+' has to appear on either side of the str().

On it's own a variable can be printed by

```
>>>print (variable)
```

At the end of a sentence:

```
>>>print (' sentence' , variable)
```

In the middle of a sentence:

```
>>>print (' sentence1' , variable, ' sentence2')
```

Assignment Operators

There are 8 types of assignment operators in Python. They are especially useful when assigning values.

i. Equal to

The symbol '=' is used to represent this operation. It is used to assign the value on the right to the variable on the left.

Example

```
>>> i = 5
      j = 10
      k = 25
```

ii. Add and

This operator is used to assign to the variable on the left. It adds the value of the variable on the left to the value on the right then assigns it to the variable on the left. The symbol used to carry out this operation '+='.

Example

```
>>> i = 5
    i += 10 # basically the expression means i =
5 + 10
    print (i)
    15
```

iii. Subtract and

This operator subtracts the value on the right from the value of the variable on the left, then assigns the result to the variable on the left. The symbol used to carry out this operation '-='.

Example

```
>>> j = 24
    j -= 10 # basically the expression means j =
24 - 10
    print (j)
    14
```

iv. Multiply and

This operator multiplies the value of the variable on the right with the value on the left, then assigns the product to the variable on the left. The symbol used to carry out this operation '*='.

Example

```
>>> k = 3
    k *= 5 # basically the expression means k =
3*5
```

```
print (k)
15
```

v. Divide and

This operator divides the value of the variable on the left by the value on the right, then assigns the quotient to the variable on the left. The symbol used to carry out this operation '/='.

Example

```
>>> l = 16
    l /= 5 # basically the expression means l =
15*5
    print (l)
    3.2
```

vi. Exponent and

This operator performs an exponential operation by raising the power of the variable on the left with the value on the right. The symbol used to carry out this operation '**='.

Example

```
>>> m = 2
    m **= 5 # basically the expression means m =
2**5
    print (m)
    32
```

vii. Modulus and

This operator divides the value of the variable on the left by the value on the right, then assigns the leftover of the division to the

variable on the left. The symbol used to carry out this operation
'%='.

Example

```
>>> n = 49
    n %= 5 # basically the expression means n%5
    print (n)
    4
```

viii.   Floor Division and

This operator divides the value of the variable on the left by the
value on the right. From the result of the division, it assigns the
whole number (without the decimal number(s)) to the variable on
the left. The symbol used to carry out this operation '//='

Example

```
>>> n = 49
    n //= 5 # basically the expression means n//5
    print (n)
    9
```

Operator	Equal to	Add and	Subtract and	Multiply and	Divide and	Exponent and	Modulus And	Floor division and
Symbol	=	+=	-=	*=	/=	**=	%=	//=

Relational or Comparison Operators.

Relational operators are used to relate the value on the left operator with the value on the right operator as either a True or False relationship. There are 6 types of relational operators.

i.   equal to

This operator checks whether the value on the right is the same as the value on the left. The symbol used to perform this operation is '=='.

Examples

```
>>> 6 == 5
    False

>>> i = 12
    J = 15
    i == j
    False

>>> j = 12
    k = 12
    j == k
    True
```

ii. less than

This operator checks whether the value on the left is less than the value on the right. The symbol used to perform this operation is '<'.

Examples

```
>>> 6 < 5
    False
```

```
>>> i = 12
    J = 15
    i < j
True

>>> j = 15
    k = 12
    j < k
False
```

iii. greater than

This operator checks whether the value on the left is greater than the value on the right. The symbol used to perform this operation is '>'.

Examples

```
>>> 6 > 5
    True

>>> i = 12
    J = 15
    i > j
    False

>>> j = 15
    k = 12
    j > k
    True
```

iv. less than or equal to

This operator checks whether the value on the left is less or equal to the value on the right. The symbol used to perform this operation is '<='.

Examples

```
>>> 11 <= 5
    False

>>> a = 22
    b = 22
    a <= b
    True

>>> y = 11
    z = 44
    y <= z
    True
```

v.   greater than or equal to

This operator checks whether the value on the left is greater or equal to the value on the right. The symbol used to perform this operation is '>='.

Examples

```
>>> 33 >= 3
    True

>>> c = 47
    d = 15
    c >= d
    True

>>> j = 2
    k = 100
    j >= k
    False
```

vi. not equal to

This operator checks whether the value on the right is different from value on the left. The symbol used to perform this operation is '!='.

Examples

```
>>> 11 != 5
    True


>>> a = 22
    b = 22
    a != b
    False


>>> y = 11
    z = 44
    y != z
    True
```

Operator	Equal to	Less than	Greater than	Less than or equal to	Greater than or equal to	Not equal to
Symbol	==	<	>	<=	>=	!=

Logical operators

Logical operators specify to the interpreter the conditions a statement can be True or False. There are three types of logical operators in Python.

- or,
- and,
- not.

i. or

If there are two operations and or is used, the operator tells the interpreter to test the correctness of the first operation and only test the second operation if the first is False.

Examples

```
>>>(8 != 2) or (8 <= 2)    """   the      first
operation is True while the second operation is
False,    but    with    the    'or'   operator    the
interpreter only tests the second operation only
when the first is False. If the second is also
False, it prints False"""
        True

    >>>(2 >= 8) or (2 == 2) # only the second
operation is True
        True
    >>>(2 >= 8) or (2 != 2) # both operations are
False
        False
```

ii. and

This operator tells the interpreter that both operations have to be True to print a True. If one of the operations is false, then Python prints False.

Examples

```
>>>(8 != 2) and (8 <= 2) # operation 2 is False
    False
>>>(2 <= 8) and (2 == 2) # both operations are
True
        True
>>>(2 >= 8) and (2 != 2) # both operations are
False
        False
```

iii. not

This operator tells the interpreter to print the opposite state of correctness of the operation.

Examples

```
>>>not(8 != 2) # operation is True
False
>>>not(2 >= 8) # operation is False
True
>>>not(2 != 2) # operation is False
True
```

Order of Python Operators

When a statement contains more than one Python operator, there's an order in which the operations will be executed. The order goes as follows:

Order	Operation	Symbol
1.	Exponentiation	**
2.	Multiplication, division, modulo, and floor division	*, /, %, //
3.	Addition and Subtraction	+, -
4.	Relational Operations	<=, <, >, >=
5.	Equality Operations	==, !=
6.	Assignment Operations	=, +=, -=, *=, /=, %=, //=, **=
7.	Logical Operations	or, and, not

Chapter 6

Conditional Statements and Loops

Conditional Statements

Condition statements are used to execute actions based on whether a condition is determined to be True or False. The use of *if-else* conditional statements or expressions is a very important part of programming; they help to shorten codes and prevent codes from being unnecessarily long. It's easier to write codes with conditi0onal statements.

Syntax of if-else statements:

> ***if condition:***
>> ***block_1_statements***
>
> ***elif condition_2:***
>> ***block_2_statements***
>
> ***else:***
>> ***block_3_statements***

if, else, and elif are Python keywords that used to write conditional statements. Logical operators are used to create the conditional statements.

Flow:

The interpreter tests *condition,* if it is true, it executes *block_1_statements.* If *condition* is false, it moves on and tests *condition_2.* A true result will lead to the execution of *block_2_statements.* If it is a false result, the interpreter will execute *block_3_statements.*

Examples

```
>>>full_name = input("Hi, can you enter your
full name? ")
    print ("Wow, your name sounds intelligent " +
name + "!")
    age = input("How old were you on your last
birthday? ")
    print("Really, you are " + age + " years old,
" + full_name + "!")
    if age == '18':
        print("Excellent, this questionnaire is for
you!")
        time = input("How many hours per day do you
spend on your smartphone?")
    elif age == '19':
print("Good, please answer this questionnaire.")
time2 = input("How many hours per day do you
spend on your system?")
        else:
        print("Thank you for filling the survey.")
        quit()
```

There are three different types of output for this program, depending on the value the user inputs.

Output 1:

```
Hi, can you enter your full name? Luke Evans
Wow, your name sounds intelligent Luke Evans!
How old were you on your last birthday?  18
Really, you are 18 years old, Luke Evans!
Excellent, this questionnaire is for you!
How many hours per day do you spend on your
smartphone? 13
```

Output 2:

```
Hi, can you enter your full name? Luke Evans
Wow, your name sounds intelligent Luke Evans!
How old were you on your last birthday?  19
Really, you are 19 years old, Luke Evans!
Good, please answer this questionnaire
How many hours per day do you spend on your
system? 9
```

Output 3:

```
Hi, can you enter your full name? Luke Evans
Wow, your name sounds intelligent Luke Evans!
How old were you on your last birthday?  12
Really, you are 12 years old, Luke Evans!
Thank you for filling the survey. # Closes the
program
```

In the first output, the *if* condition is True and the interpreter executes the *if* block statements. In the second output, the *if* condition is False and the interpreter moves on to the *elif* block. The *elif* block was tested to be True and the *elif* block statements were executed. In the third output, both the *if* and *elif* conditions were

False. The interpreter moved on to the else statement and quit the program.

Nested if statement

A nested *if* statement occurs when another *if* statement is present inside a *if* statement.

Example

```
>>> number = input (" Enter a number: ")
    if number >= 0:
      if number == 0:
            print (" Input is equal to zero " )
      else:
            print ( " Input is a positive number
" )
        else:
        print ( " Input is a negative number " )
```

Output 1:

```
Enter a number: 0
Input is equal to zero
```

Output 2:

```
Enter a number: 12
Input is a positive number
```

Output 3:

```
Enter a number: -3
Input is a negative number
```

NB: Do not forget to end the *if* statement with the symbol ':' to prevent syntax error.

Loops

Loop refers to the programming construct that controls the flow of a program. It is used to perform a set of statements repeatedly. There are 2 types of loop statements in Python, they are:

- for loop and
- while loop

The 'for' loop

The 'for' loop is used to print the items in a list in a specified order. There are two parts to the for loop: the header that specifies the item to be iterated and the body that contains the action to be executed. Usually, the for loop is used when the number of repetitions is known.

Syntax:

```
>>> for <variable> in <list>:
    # statements which require execution
```

Example

1.

```
>>>bag_brands = ['Gucci', 'Chanel', 'louis Vuitton',
'Michael Kors', 'Buscemi']
    for choice in bag_brands:
        if choice == 'Gucci':
            print('If you are choosing ' + choice)
            print ('Price is $1,800.')
        if choice == 'Chanel':
            print('If you are choosing ' + choice)
                print ('Price is $1,600.')
```

```python
    if choice == 'louis Vuitton':
        print('If you are choosing ' + choice)
        print ('Price is $2,000.')
    if choice == 'Michael Kors':
        print('If you are choosing ' + choice)
        print ('Price is $800.')
    if choice == 'Buscemi':
        print('If you are choosing ' + choice)
        print ('Price is $700.')
```

The program above is designed to be a catalogue, when it runs the following will display on your screen:

```
Thank you for selecting Gucci
Price is $1,800.
Thank you for selecting Chanel
Price is $1,600.
Thank you for selecting louis Vuitton
Price is $2,000.
Thank you for selecting Michael Kors
Price is $800.
Thank you for selecting Buscemi
Price is $700.
```

2. To print the squares of values in a list using the for loop-

```python
>>>integer = [12, 75, 87, 34, 45, 56, 67, 78, 87, 98, 54, 34, 65, 87, 42]
    square = 0
    for value in integer:
        square = value**2
        print (square)
```

The result will be:

```
    144
```

```
5625
7569
1156
2025
3136
4489
6084
7569
9604
2916
1156
4225
7569
1764
```

NB:

- You have to assign the variable 'square' a value before it can be used in the for loop.
- The ':' symbol is indispensable when writing a loop or conditional statement.

How to use the if else stement in for loop

The else statement in a for loop is used to execute a different set of command(s) if the condition(s) in the for loop is not met.

Example

```
>>>bag_brands = ('Gucci', 'Chanel', 'louis Vuitton',
'Michael Kors', 'Buscemi')
    for choice in bag_brands:
      if choice == 'Buscemi':
            print('My all-time favorite is ' + choice +
', you definitely
    have to pick this.')
```

```
        print ('Price is $1,800.')
    else:
            print('Thank you for selecting ' + choice)
            print ('Price is $1,600.')
```
The program will run as:
Thank you for selecting Gucci
Price is $1,600.
Thank you for selecting Chanel
Price is $1,600.
Thank you for selecting louis Vuitton
Price is $1,600.
Thank you for selecting Michael Kors
Price is $1,600.
My all-time favorite Buscemi, you definitely have to
pick this
Price is $1,800.

The condition set in the program is that the choice of bag has to be Buscemi. Until the condition is met, the program will keep printing the else statement.

How to use the break statement in a for loop.

The break statement directs the interpreter to end the loop and move on to the statements after the loop.

Example

```
>>>bag_brands   =   ('Gucci',   'Chanel',   'louis
Vuitton', 'Michael Kors', 'Buscemi')
    for choice in bag_brands:
if choice == 'Michael Kors':
print('My all time favorite is ' + choice + ', you
definitely
    have to pick this.')
        print ('Price is $1,800.')
```

```python
        break
    else:
        print('Thank you for selecting ' + choice)
        print ('Price is $1,600.')
print("Excellent choice, proceed to checkout.")
```

In this program, the choice has to be Micheal Kors. Once the condition is met, the loop will end(break) and the interpreter will execute the statement(s) after the loop:

```
Thank you for selecting Gucci
Price is $1,600.
Thank you for selecting Chanel
Price is $1,600.
Thank you for selecting louis Vuitton
Price is $1,600.
My   all-time   favorite   is   Michael   Kors,   you
definitely have to pick this.
Price is $1,800.
Excellent choice, proceed to checkout.
```

How to use the range() function with for loop.

You already know what the range function does, now it's time to apply it with the for loop.

Example

```python
>>>sum = 0
    for value in range(0, 35, 3):
        sum = sum + value
        print(sum)
    print('The final sum is', sum)
```

The range function used tells the interpreter to start from 0, end at 34, and move 3 numbers at a time. Upon executing, the following will display on the screen:

```
0
3
9
18
30
45
63
84
108
135
165
198
The final sum is 198
```

How to use a nested for loop

A nested for loop occurs when another for loop is present inside a for loop.

Example

```
>>>for number1 in range(5):
        for number2 in range(8, 15):
            print(number1, ",", number2)
```

Upon execution, the program will display:

```
0 , 8
0 , 9
0 , 10
0 , 11
0 , 12
```

                0 , 13
                0 , 14
                1 , 8
                1 , 9
                1 , 10
                1 , 11
                1 , 12
                1 , 13
                1 , 14
                2 , 8
                2 , 9
                2 , 10
                2 , 11
                2 , 12
                2 , 13
                2 , 14

The while loop

The while loop is used to execute a statement while the condition defined remains true. As long as the condition remains true, the loop will keep repeating. The program stops the moment the condition becomes false. Unlike the for loop, the number of iterations is not known.

Syntax of the while loop:

while condition

statements

The first thing the interpreter does is to check if the condition is true, if true, it executes the statement(s) in the body of the while loop. Then it starts again at the condition of the loop and keeps executing the command(s) until the condition turns false.

Example

```
>>>number = 0
   print('The first number is:' , number)
   while number < 10:
       number = number + 1
       print( 'The next number is:' , number )
   print ('Done with the addition, the final
number is', number)
```

The output will be:

```
The first number is: 0
The next number is: 1
The next number is: 2
The next number is: 3
The next number is: 4
The next number is: 5
The next number is: 6
The next number is: 7
The next number is: 8
The next number is: 9
The next number is: 10
Done with the addition, the final number is 10
```

How to create an infinite while loop

An infinite while loop occurs when the condition continues to remain true infinitely.

Example

```
>>>number = 1
   while number < 5:
       print(True)
The output will be:
True
```

```
True
True
True
True
True
True
True......
```

The program will keep running till you close the window because the condition will always remain true.

Nested while loop

A nested while loop occurs when another while loop is present inside a while loop.

Example

```
>>>l = 0
    m = 2
    while l < 4:
        while m < 8:
            print(l, ",", m)
            m = m + 1
            l = l + 1
```

The output will be:

```
0 , 2
1 , 3
2 , 4
3 , 5
4 , 6
5 , 7
```

Chapter 7

Python Data Types Continued

Lists

Lists are used to store data in Python. It is a data type that can store several other data types such as strings, integers, and objects. Lists are very powerful as they can hold more than one data type at once and can be modified at any point after creation. They perform the same function as an array in other programming languages. Lists are ordered and have a specific count, hence, each element in a list has its own specific spot. Knowledge of how to create, use, and manipulate a list is crucial to a data scientist whose main job is to analyze and extract data. Every single thing you need to know about a list is covered in this chapter.

How to Create a List

A list is created by arranging items in brackets' [ ]'. A value can be repeated more than once because they all have their distinct location in the list.

```python
# Python program that shows how to create a list
# simple list creation
simple_list = [ ]
print ("Initial empty List: ")
print ( simple_list )

# how to create a List with the using a String
string_list = ['DataScienceFromScratch']
```

```python
print ("\nList created with a String: ")
print ( string_list )

# how to create a List that holds multiple
values
multi_list   =   ["Data",   "Science",   "From",
"Scratch"]
print("\nList that holds multiple values: ")
print( multi_list[0] )  #to print the first item
in the list
print( multi_list[1] )  #to print the second item
in the list

print( multi_list[2] )  #to print the third item
in the list
print( multi_list[3] )  #to print the fourth item
in the list

# how to create a Multi-Dimensional List By
placing another list inside a List)
multiD_list = [ ['Data', 'Science'] , ['From'] ,
['Scratch'] ]
print("\n The Multi-Dimensional List: ")
print ( multiD_list)

# how to create a List with Numbers and repeated
values
num_list = [1, 5, 7, 2, 8, 8, 8, 6, 3]
print("\nList with the repeated Numbers: ")
print ( num_list )

# how to create a List with different data
types: strings and numbers
variety_list = [1, 5, 'Data', 8, 'Science', 6,
'From' , 3, 'Scratch']
```

```python
print("\nList with different data types: ")
print (variety_list)
```

The output of the program above:

```
Initial empty List:
[]

List created with a String:
['DataScienceFromScratch']

List that holds multiple values:
Data
Science
From
Scratch

The Multi-Dimensional List:
[['Data', 'Science'], ['From'], ['Scratch']]

List with the repeated Numbers:
[1, 5, 7, 2, 8, 8, 8, 6, 3]

List with different data types:
[1, 5, 'Data', 8, 'Science', 6, 'From', 3,
'Scratch']
```

The program above is self-explanatory. Different lists were created using different data types.

NB: '\n' is used to start a new line in Python.

How to Add Elements to a List

append() is a built-in function used to add elements to the bottom of a list. With the append() function, you can only add one element at a time. The extend() function is used to add more than one element at once to the bottom of a list. If the append() function is used in a loop, it's possible to add more than one element at once. To add an element at any particular point in a list the insert() function is used.

```python
# Python program that demonstrates how to add
elements to a List
# Create an empty List
empty_list = [ ]
print(" Initial empty List: " )
print ( empty_list )

# add elements to the bottom of the list
empty_list.append(5)
empty_list.append(8)
empty_list.append(11)
empty_list.append(15)
print ("\nList after Adding Four Elements: ")
print ( empty_list )

# how to add elements to a list using a loop
for j in range(4, 10):
        empty_list.append( j )
print ("\nList after Adding elements from 4-10:
")
print ( empty_list)

# Adding a List to another List
filled_list = ['Data', 'Science']
empty_list.append( filled_list )
```

```python
print ("\nList after Adding Elements from
another List: ")
print ( empty_list )

# Adding Elements to a particular Position using
insert() function
# remember numbering of all list start from
position 0
empty_list.insert(6, 15)       # this adds 15 to
postion 6 in the list
filled_list.insert(2, 'From') # this adds from
to postion 2 in the list
print ("\nList after using insert() function: ")
print ( empty_list)

# Adding multiple elements to the bottom of a
list with extend function
empty_list.extend([ 'Scratch', 'Beginners'])
print ("\nList after using the extend()
function: ")
print ( empty_list )
```

Output :

```
Intial empty list:
[]
List after Adding Four Elements:
[5, 8, 11, 15]

List after Adding elements from 4-10:
[5, 8, 11, 15, 4, 5, 6, 7, 8, 9]

List after Adding another List:
[5, 8, 11, 15, 4, 5, 6, 7, 8, 9, ['Data',
'Science']]
```

```
List after using insert() function:
[5, 8, 11, 15, 4, 5, 15, 6, 7, 8, 9, ['Data',
'Science', 'From']]

List after using the extend() function:
[5, 8, 11, 15, 4, 5, 15, 6, 7, 8, 9, ['Data',
'Science', 'From'], 'Scratch', 'Beginners']
```

How to Access an Element in a List

Like strings, the index of a list starts with 0. To select a particular item in a list, you have to enclose its index number with brackets []. For nested lists, you have to use double brackets [ ] [ ], with the first bracket containing the index of the list you want to access and the second bracket containing the index of the item in the list.

```python
# Python program that demonstrates how to access
an element from the list
# Create a List with multiple values
multi_list   =   ["Data",   "Science",   "From",
"Scratch" ]
# access an element from a list with the index
number
print (" Elements from the list: ")
print ( multi_list[0])
print ( multi_list[1])
print ( multi_list[2])


# Create a Multi-Dimensional List by nesting a
list inside another List)
multiD_list = [['Data', 'Science'] , ['From'],
['Scratch']]


# Print an element from a Multi-Dimensional List
with the index number
```

```python
print (" Access elements in a Multi-Dimensional
list: ")
print ( multiD_list[0][1])
print ( multiD_list[1][0])

multi_list = [9, 8, 'Data', 7, 'Science', 5,
'From', 'Scratch']
# how to use the negative index to access an
element in a list
print ( "Access an element with negative index:"
)
print( multi_list[-1]) #this will print the
element in the list
print(multi_list[-3])  # this will print the
third to the last element
```

Output:

```
Elements from the list:
Data
Science
From
Access elements in a Multi-Dimensional list:
Science
From
Access an element with negative index:
Scratch
5
```

How to Remove an Element from a List

remove() function is used to delete an element in a list. It can only remove one element at a time. When the remove() function is used in a loop, it can be used to remove multiple elements. In addition, the pop() function can be used to remove elements at a particular position.

```python
# Python program that demonstrates the removal
of elements in a List
# Create a List
s_list = [ 'my', 'baby', 'cat', 'ate', 'a',
'big', 'meal', 1, 2, 'before', 'it', 'slept' ]
print ( "Intial s_list: " )
print ( s_list )


# using the remove method to remove elements in
a list
s_list.remove( 1)
s_list.remove( 2 )
print ("\n List after removing two elements: ")
print ( s_list )


# Removing multiple elements with remove()
function in the for loop
s_list = [ 1, 2, 3, 4, 5, 6, 7, 8, 9, 10, 11,
12]
for i in range( 1, 3 ):
    s_list.remove ( i )
print ("\n List after Removing a range of
elements: ")
print ( s_list )


# how to remove elements in a list with the
pop() function
s_list.pop( )
print ("\nList after popping an item in a list:
")
print ( s_list)
```

```python
# to remove an element from a particular
location in a list using the pop() function
s_list.pop(  )
print ("\nList after popping a specific element:
")
print ( s_list)
```

Output:

```
Intial s_list:
['my', 'baby', 'cat', 'ate', 'a', 'big', 'meal',
1, 2, 'before', 'it', 'slept']

List after removing two elements:
['my', 'baby', 'cat', 'ate', 'a', 'big', 'meal',
'before', 'it', 'slept']

List after Removing a range of elements:
[3, 4, 5, 6, 7, 8, 9, 10, 11, 12]

List after popping an item in a list:
[3, 4, 5, 6, 7, 8, 9, 10, 11]

List after popping a specific element:
[3, 4, 5, 6, 7, 8, 9, 10]
```

How to Slice a List

Slice operation in Python is carried out with brackets '[ ]' and colon ':'. It is used to print elements in a particular order.

```python
# Python program that demonstrates the slicing
of elements in a List
# Create a List
```

```python
D_List           =           ['D','A','T','A','S','C',
'I','E','N','C','E','F','R',
'O','M','S','C','R','A','T','C','H']
print ("Intial List: ")
print ( D_List)

# Perform slicing
slice_list = D_List[5:10] # start printing from
the 6th element to the 10th element
print ("\n Slicing elements in a range 5-10: ")
print ( slice_list )

# Print elements from beginning to a particular
spot with splicing
slice_list = D_List[:-4]
print ("\n Elements are sliced to the 4th
element from last: ")
print ( slice_list )

# Print elements from a particular starting
point to end
slice_list = D_List[7:]
print ("\n Elements are sliced from the 7th "
"element to the end: ")
print ( slice_list )

# to print elements from beginning to the end
slice_list = D_List[:]
print ("\nPrinting all elements using slice
operation: ")
print ( slice_list )

# Printing elements in reverse
# using Slice operation
Sliced_List = List[::-1]
```

```
print("\nPrinting List in reverse: ")
print(Sliced_List)
```

The output of the program above:

```
Intial List:
['D', 'A', 'T', 'A', 'S', 'C', 'I', 'E', 'N',
'C', 'E', 'F', 'R', 'O', 'M', 'S', 'C', 'R',
'A', 'T', 'C', 'H']


 Slicing elements in a range 5-10:
['C', 'I', 'E', 'N', 'C']


 Elements are sliced to the 4th element from
last:
['D', 'A', 'T', 'A', 'S', 'C', 'I', 'E', 'N',
'C', 'E', 'F', 'R', 'O', 'M', 'S', 'C', 'R']


Elements are sliced from the 7th element to the
end:
['E', 'N', 'C', 'E', 'F', 'R', 'O', 'M', 'S',
'C', 'R', 'A', 'T', 'C', 'H']


Printing all elements using slice operation:
['D', 'A', 'T', 'A', 'S', 'C', 'I', 'E', 'N',
'C', 'E', 'F', 'R', 'O', 'M', 'S', 'C', 'R',
'A', 'T', 'C', 'H']
```

A good data scientist should know how to create, add, remove, and manipulate lists in any form. It lessens the stress involved in extracting data and makes it easier and faster.

Tuples

Tuples are very similar to lists. They are also used to store data and can hold multiple data types at once. However, there are two major differences between lists and tuples. A tuple is delimited with parentheses ( ) not square brackets [ ] and it cannot be modified after it's created. Once a tuple is created, it holds the same value forever until it's deleted.

How to Create a Tuple

A tuple doesn't necessarily have to be created with parentheses, when it is not it is known as Tuple Packing. While it's possible for a tuple to hold only one item, such a tuple is very delicate to create because the comma that separates each item is also needed to make a tuple a tuple.

Examples

```python
# Python program that demonstrates how to create
a tuple
# to create a blank tuple
Blank_tuple = ( )
print ( "Initial Blank Tuple: " )
print ( Blank_tuple )

# to create a Tuple that contains a String
Filled_tuple1 = ( 'Data', 'Science', 'From',
'Scratch' )
print ( "\nTuple with the use of String: " )
print ( Filled_tuple1 )

# to create a Tuple that contains a list
Blist = [ 9, 8, 7, 6, 5, 4, 3, 2, 1 ]
print ("\nTuple using List: ")
```

```python
print (tuple( Blist ))

# to create a Tuple with a for loop
Filled_tuple2 = ( 'Data' )
num = 6
print ("\nTuple with a loop:")
for i in range (int( num )):
        Filled_tuple2 = ( Filled_tuple2, )
# the comma is necessary to create a tuple with
a single element
        print ( Filled_tuple2 )
# to create a Tuple with the tuple() built-in
function
Filled_tuple3 = tuple( 'Scratch' )
print    ("\nTuple    with    the    use    of    tuple()
function: ")
print ( Filled_tuple3 )

# to create a Tuple with Multiple Datatypes
Filled_tuple4 = ( 4, 'From', 9, 'Scratch')
print ("\nTuple with Multiple Datatypes: ")
print ( Filled_tuple4 )

# to join multiple tuples
Filled_tuple5 = ( 0, 1, 2, 3)
Filled_tuple6 = ( 'python', 'lover!' )
Filled_tuple7 = ( Filled_tuple5, Filled_tuple6 )
print("\nTuple with nested tuples: ")
print ( Filled_tuple7 )
```

The output of the program above:

```
Initial Blank Tuple:
()
```

```
Tuple with the use of String:
('Data', 'Science', 'From', 'Scratch')

Tuple using List:
(9, 8, 7, 6, 5, 4, 3, 2, 1)

Tuple with a loop:
('Data',)
(('Data',),)
((('Data',),),)
(((('Data',),),),)
((((('Data',),),),),)
(((((('Data',),),),),),)

Tuple with the use of tuple() function:
('s', 'c', 'r', 'a', 't', 'c', 'h')
Tuple with Multiple Datatypes:
(4, 'From', 9, 'Scratch')

Tuple with nested tuples:
((0, 1, 2, 3), ('python', 'lover!'))
```

Concatenation and Repition of Tuples

Concatenation joins two or more tuples together. It is carried out with the addition operator '+'. When joined, the second tuple starts exactly where the first stops to form a longer tuple. Repitition involves the multiplication of a tuple for a specified number of times and joining the resulting tuples together to form one tuple. Repitition is carried out with the multiply operator '*'.

```
# program that demonstrates how to concatenate
and repeat tuples
Tuple_a = ( 0, -1, -2, -3)
```

```python
Tuple_b = ( 'Data', 'Science', 'From', 'Sratch'
)
Tuple_c= Tuple_a + Tuple_b     # Concatenation of
tuples
print ( " 1st Tuple: " )
print ( Tuple_a )
print ("\n 2nd Tuple: ")
print ( Tuple_b )
print ("\n The Tuples after Concatenating: ")
print (Tuple_c)
Tuple_d = ('Data',) * 3
print ("\n Tuple after repetition: ")
print (Tuple_d)
```

The output of the program

```
1st Tuple:
(0, -1, -2, -3)

 2nd Tuple:
('Data', 'Science', 'From', 'Sratch')

 The Tuples after Concatenating:
(0,  -1,  -2,  -3,  'Data',  'Science',  'From',
'Sratch')

 Tuple after repetition:
('Data', 'Data', 'Data')
```

How to Slice a Tuple

Slicing is done to print specific parts of a tuple. It is done with the index number of the character, a colon':', and square brackets [ ].

N.B: In python, index number starts from zero at the beginning and -1 at the ending.

```python
# a program that demonstrates how to slice a
Tuple
# Slicing a Tuple with positive index
Tuple_a = tuple ('DATASCIENCE')
print ( "Removal of the First character: " )
print ( Tuple_a[1:] )

# reversing the elements
print ("\n Printing the reverse elements: ")
print (Tuple_a[::-1]) # notice the double colons

# Printing elements with range()
print("\n Printing elements between Range 3-8: ")
print ( Tuple_a[3:8])   # no use of a comma this
time
```

Output:

```
Removal of the First character:
('A', 'T', 'A', 'S', 'C', 'I', 'E', 'N', 'C',
'E')

 Printing the reverse elements:
('E', 'C', 'N', 'E', 'I', 'C', 'S', 'A', 'T',
'A', 'D')

 Printing elements between Range 3-8:
('A', 'S', 'C', 'I', 'E')
```

How to use Tuple for Multiple Assignment Operations

A tuple can be used to assign values to multiple variables with a single statement. This is called multiple assignment. To perform this operation, the tuple can be combined with a function. For example:

```python
a, b = 10, 20                # a is 10 and b 20
print (' The value of a is: ' +str(a))
print (' The value of b is: ' +str(b))
# to swap the values of variables
a, b = b, a            # a is now 20 and b 10
print (' The value of a is: ' +str(a))
print (' The value of b is: ' +str(b))
# combination of tuple and function for multiple
assignment
def product_and_sum( c,d ):       # defining the
function of product_and_sum
     return  ( c*d ),( c+d )
mn = product_and_sum (3, 4)    # calling  on  the
function
print (' The value of mn is: ' +str(mn))
m, n = product_and_sum( 5, 10)
print (' The value of m and n are: ' +str(m) + '
and ' +str(n))
```

The output:

```
The value of a is: 10
 The value of b is: 20
 The value of a is: 20
 The value of b is: 10
 The value of mn is: (12, 7)
 The value of m and n are: 50 and 15
```

How to Delete a Tuple

It's not possible to delete or edit just a part of a tuple. To delete a part of a tuple, you have to delete the entire tuple. This is done with the del() function. You cannot use or print the tuple again after it's deleted, you will have to create another tuple that contains your desired content.

Example

```
Tuple_a = ( 0, 1, 2, 3, 4 )
del Tuple_a
print ( Tuple_a )
```

Output:

```
Traceback (most recent call last):
  File "C:/Python27/Lib/idlelib/nc.py", line 3,
in <module>
    print ( Tuple_a )
NameError: name 'Tuple_a' is not defined
```

As you can see, once a tuple is deleted, calling on it or trying to access it will result in an error.

Sets

Sets are unordered collections of data type. Unlike list, when you store data in a set, it doesn't retain the order. Sets do not hold duplicate elements and can be edited at any time.

The mathematical sets and the Python sets are very much identical. They both undergo union, intersection, and difference operations. Python sets have the fastest method to check for the presence of an element in it.

How to Create a Set

The set( ) function is used to create a set. It doesn't retain the order of creation and can only contain unique items. Though, at the point of creation, it will accept duplicate elements. Like in mathematics, when the elements in a set are printed they are separated with commas and surrounded with curly braces. There's no particular order to the elements when printed and it's not possible to rearrange them. Though it can contain multiple data types at the same time, the data will end up shuffled.

NB: A set cannot contain another set, list, and dictionary.

```python
# program that demonstrates how to create
different types of set
# Creating an empty Set
set_a = set( )
print ( "Intial Empty Set: " )
print ( set_a )

# how to create a Set that contains a String
set_a = set( "DataScienceFromScratch" )
print ( "\n Set containing a String: " )
print ( set_a )

# how to create a set with a Constructor
String = 'DataScienceFromScratch'
set_a = set( String )
print ( "\n Set with a Constructor: " )
print ( set_a )

# how to creating a Set with with a List
set_a = set( [ "Data", "Science", "From",
"Scratch" ] )
print ( "\n Set created with a List: " )
print ( set_a )

# how to create a Set that contains numbers with
duplicate values
set_a = set( [1, 7, 5, 2, 9, 5, 4, 0, 1, 8, 3,
4, 3, 5, 3, 3, 4, 6, 5] )
print ( "\n Set with duplicate Numbers: " )
```

```python
print ( set_a )

# how to create a Set that contains multiple
data types
# (Having numeric data types and strings)
set_a = set( [ 1, 2, 'Data', 4, 5, 6, 'Science',
1, 3, 9, 'From', 4, 3, 6, 'Scratch' ] )
print ( "\n Set with the use of Mixed Values: "
)
print ( set_a )
```

Output:

```
Intial Empty Set:
set()

Set containing a String:
{'m', 't', 'a', 'i', 'e', 'n', 'o', 'h', 'D',
'c', 'F', 'r', 'S'}

Set with a Constructor:
{'m', 't', 'a', 'i', 'e', 'n', 'o', 'h', 'D',
'c', 'F', 'r', 'S'}

Set created with a List:
{'Scratch', 'Data', 'Science', 'From'}
Set with duplicate Numbers:

{0, 1, 2, 3, 4, 5, 6, 7, 8, 9}
Set with the use of Mixed Values:

{1, 2, 'Data', 4, 5, 6, 'Science', 3, 9,
'Scratch', 'From'}
```

As you can see, the order in which the elements are stored into set is quite different from the order that ends up being printed. There's no way to predict how the interpreter will print the data present in a set, it's best to use a list or tuple if you have to store data in a particular order. The next objective is to learn how to add, delete, add, and edit sets in different ways.

How to Modify a Set

The built-in add() function is used to add elements to a set. You can only add a single element when using the add() function except when it is combined with a for loop. With the for loop the add() function can add as many elements as needed. Without the for loop the only way to add multiple elements at once is with the update() function.   The update function can add tuples and strings as elements because they cannot be modified. Lists can also be added but not as elements because they can be edited. However, the most important thing to note in all three cases is that the addition of duplicate elements must be avoided at all cost. Duplicate elements are accepted when creating a set but not when modifying, all elements must be unique when updating or adding to a set. Duplicate elements will lead to an error when the interpreter runs through the program.

The remove() function is used to delete elements in a set. If that particular element does not exist in the set, a KeyError will occur and the program will stop running. To prevent an interruption in the running of the program, discard( ) function can be used. It will remove the element if it exists, and if it does not it allow the program to continue running without a hitch. The pop() function used to delete elements in lists is also used to delete elements in sets, and it can only remove an element at a time, starting from the bottom. To erase or completely remove all the elements in a set, the clear() function is used.

NB: Because a set is disordered it's not possible to know which element will be deleted by the pop() function. The best option is to use a method that allows you to specify the element to remove.

```python
# Python program that demonstrate how to Add and
remove elements from a Set
# Create an empty Set
set_a = set( )
print ( "Intial Empty Set: " )
print ( set_a )

# Add an element to the empty Set
set_a.add( 7 )
set_a.add( 3 )
set_a.add( 15 )
set_a.add( 19 )
print ( "\n Set after Adding Four elements: " )
print ( set_a )

# Adding elements to aSet with a for loop
for i in range(3, 9):
        set_a.add(i)
print ( "\n Set after Adding elements from 3-9:
" )
print ( set_a )

# how to Add a Tuple to a Set
set_a.add( ( 9, 11 ) )
print ( "\n Set after Adding a Tuple: " )
print ( set_a )
```

```python
# Adding elements to the Set with Update
function
set_a.update( [ 15, 19 ] )
print ( "\n Set after Adding elements with the
Update function: " )
print ( set_a )

# removing elements from a set with the Remove(
) function
set_a.remove( 5 )
set_a.remove( 15 )
print ( "\n Set after removing two elements: " )
print ( set_a )

# Removing elements from a Set with the
Discard() function
set_a.discard( 11 )
set_a.discard( 9 )
print ( "\nSet after Discarding two elements: "
)
print ( set_a )

# how to Remove elements from Set with the for
loop
for i in range( 3, 4  ):
        set_a.remove(i)
print ( "\nSet after Removing a range of
elements: " )
print ( set_a )

# how to delete an element from a Set with the
pop() function
set_a.pop()
print ( "\nSet after using pop( ) function: " )
print ( set_a )
```

```python
# how to remove all the elements in a Set with
the clear( ) function
set_a.clear( )
print ("\nSet after clearing all the elements:
")
print ( set_a )
```

The full output of the program above:

```
Initial Empty Set:
set()

Set after Adding Four elements:
{19, 3, 15, 7}

Set after Adding elements from 3-9:
{3, 4, 5, 6, 7, 8, 15, 19}

Set after Adding a Tuple:
{3, 4, 5, 6, 7, 8, 15, 19, (9, 11)}

Set after Adding elements with the Update
function:
{3, 4, 5, 6, 7, 8, 15, 19, (9, 11)}

Set after removing two elements:
{3, 4, 6, 7, 8, 19, (9, 11)}

Set after Discarding two elements:
{3, 4, 6, 7, 8, 19, (9, 11)}

Set after Removing a range of elements:
{4, 6, 7, 8, 19, (9, 11)}
```

```
Set after using pop( ) function:
{6, 7, 8, 19, (9, 11)}

Set after clearing all the elements:
set( )
```

Frozen Sets

Frozen sets are sets that can no longer be modified. They do not
respond to add(), remove(), pop() or any other function that applies
to set. However, they can be printed but the item to be printed has to
be specified in the print statement.

Examples

```
# Python program that demonstrates how FrozenSet
works

# Create a Set

Set_a = ('D', 'a', 't', 'a', 'S', 'c', 'i', 'e',
'n', 'c', 'e' )

Frozenset_a = frozenset( Set_a )
print ( "The FrozenSet is: " )
print ( Frozenset_a )

# To print blank Frozen Set, the set name isn't
specified
print ( "\n Empty FrozenSet: " )
print ( frozenset( ) )
```

Output:

```
The FrozenSet is:
```

```
frozenset({'t', 'i', 'c', 'S', 'a', 'n', 'D',
'e'})
Empty FrozenSet:
frozenset()
```

Dictionaries

Like set, the dictionary is an unordered collection of data and it can contain multiple data types at once. What distinguishes Python dictionaries from other data types is its ability to link one data type to another. It works like a map in which you store a particular value inside a location. The location and the value of dictionaries are called the 'key-value' pair. A real-life dictionary is also a good example of how a Python dictionary works. The words that are defined are the *keys* and the definitions are the *values*. Just as a word can have different meanings, a key can contain different values.

The values in a key can be modified but the key that holds a value can't be changed. While a key can hold identical values, the key itself must be unique and be of a data type that is uneditable like tuples, Integers, and Strings.

How to Create a Dictionary

The key-value pair is created with a colon ':' in between them and a comma separating them from other elements. The chain of elements are enclosed in curly braces '{ }'. The elements in a dictionary can be of any data type and they can be altered at any point.

An empty dictionary is created with blank curly braces { }. A dictionary can also be created with the built-in dict( ) function.

NB: Python is case sensitive and two dictionaries with the same name in different levels of capitalization have different meanings in Python.

```python
# Python program that demonstrates how to create
a blank Dictionary
Emp_dict = { }
print ( " Blank Dictionary: " )
print ( Emp_Dict )


# to create a dictionary with integers as keys
Emp_Dict  =  {4:  'Data',  7:  'Scratch',  8:
'Science'}
print ( "\nDictionary with the use of Integer
Keys: " )
print ( Emp_Dict )


# to create a dictionary with keys of different
data types
Emp_Dict = { 'Book': 'Data', 1: [1, 2, 3, 4] }
        #book is the first key and 1 is the second
key
print ( "\nDictionary with the use of Mixed
Keys: " )
print ( Emp_Dict )


# to create a Dictionary with dict() function
Emp_Dict  =  dict(  {  1:  'Data',  2:  'For',
3:'Science' } )
print ( "\nDictionary with the use of dict(): "
)
print ( Emp_Dict )


# to create a Dictionary with each item as a
Pair
```

```python
Emp_Dict = dict( [ ( 1, 'Data' ), ( 2, 'For' ) ]
)
print ( "\nDictionary with each item as a pair:
" )
print ( Emp_Dict )

# to creating a Nested Dictionary as shown in
the below image
Emp_Dict = {1: 'Data', 2: 'Science',
            3:{ 'A' : 'From', 'B' : 'Beginners',
'C' : 'Scratch' } }
print ( Emp_Dict )
```

The output of the program above:

```
Blank Dictionary:
{}

Dictionary with the use of Integer Keys:
{8: 'Science', 4: 'Data', 7: 'Scratch'}

Dictionary with the use of Mixed Keys:
{1: [1, 2, 3, 4], 'Book': 'Data'}

Dictionary with the use of dict():
{1: 'Data', 2: 'For', 3: 'Science'}

Dictionary with each item as a pair:
{1: 'Data', 2: 'For'}

{1: 'Data', 2: 'Science', 3: {'A': 'From', 'C':
'Scratch', 'B': 'Beginners'}}
```

How to add to, access, and delete elements in a dictionary?

There are various ways to add elements to a dictionary. You can add one value at a time by specifying the key you want to edit and value you want to add e.g dict [Key] = 'Value'. The value will be added to the key immediately but if the value already exists, a new key will be created to contain the value-added. To replace a value present inside a key, the update( ) function is used.

To call on or access the elements in a dictionary, you have to refer to its key name. The key name should be written in square brackets [ ]. The get( ) function can also retrieve an element in a dictionary.

Deletion of keys in a dictionary is done with del( ) function, pop( ) function, and popitem( ) function. del() function is only used to remove specific keys, it can't delete randomly or in a specific order. For that, the pop( ) and pop( ) item function is used. clear() function is used to delete all keys in a dictionary at once.

NB: The del (Dict_name) will also delete the dictionary totally, it will no longer be available for printing.

Example 1

```
# Python program that demonstrates how to add
elements to a dictionary
# Create a blank Dictionary
Dictry = {}
print ( "Empty Dictionary: " )
print ( Dictry )

#how to add elements one after another
Dictry[0] = 'Data'
Dictry[1] = 'Science'
```

```python
Dictry[2] = 'From'
Dictry[3] = 'Scratch'
print ( "\nDictionary after adding 3 elements: "
)
print ( Dictry )


# How to Add set of values to a particular Key
Dictry ['Value_set'] = 2, 3, 4
print ( "\nDictionary after adding 3 elements to
a key: " )
print ( Dictry )


# how to Update an existing Key's Value
Dictry[3] = 'Beginners'
print ( "\n Updated key value: " )
print ( Dictry )


# how to Add a Nested Key value to a Dictionary
Dictry[5] = { 'Nested' :{'3' : 'Scratch', '4' :
'Data' } }
print ( "\nAdding a Nested Key: " )
print ( Dictry )
```

Example 2

```python
# Python program that demonstrates how to access
an element from a Dictionary
# Create a Dictionary

Dictry_a = {1: 'Data', 'Scratch': 'From', 3:
'Science'}


# to access an element with a key
print ( "Acessing an element with a key:" )
```

```python
print ( Dictry_a['Scratch'] )                    #    to
print 'scratch' key from the dictionary
print ("Acessing an element with a key:")
print ( Dictry_a[3] )

# to access an element with get() function
print ( "Acessing a element using get:" )
print ( Dictry_a.get(1) )

#deleting from a dictionary
# Initial Dictionary
Dictry_b = { 5 : 'Beginners', 6 : 'From', 7 :
'Data',
            'X' : {1 : 'Data', 2 : 'Scratch', 3 :
'Science'},
            'Y' : {1 : 'Python', 2 : 'Book'} }
print ( "Initial Dictionary: " )
print ( Dictry_b )

# to Delete an entire key
del Dictry_b[ 5 ]
print ( "\nDeleting a specific key: " )
print ( Dictry_b )

# to Delete a Key from a Nested Dictionary
del Dictry_b[ 'Y' ][ 2 ]
print ( "\n Deleting a key from a Nested
Dictionary: " )
print ( Dictry_b )

# to Delete a Key with pop( ) function
Dictry_b.pop( 7 )
print ( "\nPopping specific element: " )
print ( Dictry_b )
```

```python
# to delete a key with popitem( ) function
Dictry_b.popitem( )
print ( "\nPops first element: " )
print ( Dictry_b )

# to delete an entire Dictionary
Dictry_b.clear( )
print ( "\nDeleting Entire Dictionary: " )
print ( Dictry_b )
```

The output of the two programs above:

```
Empty Dictionary:
{ }


Dictionary after adding 3 elements:
{ 0:  'Data',  1:  'Science',  2:  'From',  3:
'Scratch' }


Dictionary after adding 3 elements to a key:
{ 0:  'Data',  1:  'Science',  2:  'From',  3:
'Scratch', 'Value_set': (2, 3, 4) }


 Updated key value:
{ 0:  'Data',  1:  'Science',  2:  'From',  3:
'Beginners', 'Value_set': (2, 3, 4) }


Adding a Nested Key:
{ 0:  'Data',  1:  'Science',  2:  'From',  3:
'Beginners', 5: {'Nested': {'3': 'Scratch', '4':
'Data'}}, 'Value_set': (2, 3, 4) }
Acessing an element with a key:
From
Acessing an element with a key:
Science
```

Acessing a element using get:
Data
Initial Dictionary:
{ 'Y': {1: 'Python', 2: 'Book'}, 'X': {1: 'Data', 2: 'Scratch', 3: 'Science'}, 5: 'Beginners', 6: 'From', 7: 'Data' }

Deleting a specific key:
{ 'Y': {1: 'Python', 2: 'Book'}, 'X': {1: 'Data', 2: 'Scratch', 3: 'Science'}, 6: 'From', 7: 'Data' }

 Deleting a key from a Nested Dictionary:
{ 'Y': {1: 'Python'}, 'X': {1: 'Data', 2: 'Scratch', 3: 'Science'}, 6: 'From', 7: 'Data' }
Popping specific element:

{ 'Y': {1: 'Python'}, 'X': {1: 'Data', 2: 'Scratch', 3: 'Science'}, 6: 'From' }

Pops first element:
{ 'X': {1: 'Data', 2: 'Scratch', 3: 'Science'}, 6: 'From' }
Deleting Entire Dictionary:
{ }

Chapter 8

Modules and Exceptions

Modules

Some features of Python do not load automatically, to access them you have to import the modules they are stored in. Modules are files that contain codes, definitions, and statements.

How to Create, Name, and Save a Module

A module can be a class, function, and variable. To create a module you have to define what it will contain and save it.

Examples

```
1.    def multiply( c, d ):
      product=c * d
      return product


2.   def print_function( sentence ):
        print "Hi : ", sentence
        return


3.    constantX = 15
      constantY = 32
```

After defining the parameters of the module you have to save it as a .py file on your system. It's best to save the module with a name that relates to what the module does. For Example 1 above, the name that best fits the module is 'multiply.py', 'print_func' fits Example 2, and 'constant' for Example 3. You must not use a Python keyword to name a module to prevent errors while running the program.

How to Import and Use a Module

It is quite easy to import a module once it's saved to your system. To import a module, you use the Python keyword 'import':

```
>>> import multiply
>>> import print_func
>>> import constant
```

To use the function defined in a module, you have to use the dot '.' operator to access it:

```
>>>multiply.multiply( 3,5)
>>>print_func.print_function( " I'm Luke Evans ")
>>>print constantY
>>>print (" The value of constant X = " ,
constant.constantX )
```

Output:

```
15
Hi :  I'm Luke Evans
32
(' The value of constant X = ', 15)
```

When you install Python, you gain access to tons of modules. You can find them in the Lib directory of the Python program file installed. An example of an existing module is the 'math' module:

```
>>> import math
```

```
>>> print (" The real value of pi is " , math.pi
)
```

Output:

```
(' The real value of pi is', 3.141592653589793)
```

Exceptions

As a beginner, a lot of errors are bound to happen in the course of running your codes. The moment the interpreter encounters an error, it terminates the program. There are two possible errors that can occur, a syntax error and an exception. A syntax error is caused when a command statement is not written in the correct format. For example,

```
Dictry = { }
print ( "Empty Dictionary: " )
print ( Dictry ))
SyntaxError: invalid syntax
```

The error was caused by the incorrect print statement in the 3rd line. An exception occurs when a properly constructed command statement results in an error. For an exception, the interpreter prints a Traceback in the window. These Tracebacks show you exactly where the error originated. For example,

```
Traceback (most recent call last):
  File "C:/Python27/Lib/idlelib/bs.py", line 67,
in <module>
    Dictry_b.pop( 5 )
KeyError: 5
```

This traceback tells you that the error originated in the 67th line and was caused due to the absence of key 5 in the dictionary Dictry_b.

Creating an Exception

It's possible to envelop an exception in the middle of your code to prevent it from running if your conditions are not satisfied. The *raise* keyword combined with a conditional statement is used to accomplish this. For example,

```
a = 13
b = 21
x = a + b
if x > 5:
    raise Exception('x should not exceed 5. The value of x was: {}'.format(x))
print ( " The value of x is less than 5. " )
```

The output of the program:

```
Traceback (most recent call last):
  File "C:\Python27\Lib\idlelib\bs.py", line 5, in <module>
    raise Exception('x should not exceed 5. The value of x was: {}'.format(x))
Exception: x should not exceed 5. The value of x was: 34
```

If the value of x was less than 5, the interpreter automatically runs the print statement. The *assert* keyword can also be used to throw an exception if the condition stipulated is not met. It doesn't need a conditional statement to achieve its purpose. For example,

```
a = 13
b = 21
x = a + b
assert x == 5, ' x must be equal to 5'
print ( " The value of x is 5. " )
```

Output:

```
Traceback (most recent call last):
  File "C:\Python27\Lib\idlelib\bs.py", line 4,
in <module>
    assert x == 5, ' x must be equal to 5'
AssertionError:  x must be equal to 5
```

If x was equal to 5, the entire program would run and print:

```
The value of x is 5.
```

Handling Exceptions

Exceptions in Python can be caught and handled with a try and except statement. The try statement is a separate block from the except block. The try block contains the normal program to be executed while the except block contains the alternative program(s) to be executed if an exception occurs.

```
import sys
a = 13
b = 21
c = a + b
try:
    print ( x )
    print ( " x is less or equal to 5 " )
except:
    print("Oops!",sys.exc_info()[0],"occured.")
    print ( " x is not defined. " )
 Output:
('Oops!',      <type      'exceptions.NameError'>,
'occured.')
 x is not defined.
```

The program about caught the NameError exception and handled it by executing the statements in the except block. A lot of programmers and data scientists use exceptions to make their program cleaner, it catches errors and allows the program to run without a snag.

Part 2

Exception rounds up the crash course on Python (Python 101). The next aspect of this book uses the programming methods and techniques taught in Python 101 to analyze data and solve problems related to Data Science. The topics covered in the next section include Statistics, Probability, and Machine learning. The topics will require background knowledge in calculus, at the very least to an undergraduate level. While the calculus needed is not so complicated, reading the next part with no previous knowledge of calculus will result in minimal understanding.

Chapter 9

Data Mining

A data scientist needs data! The extraction and conversion of data into useful information is known as data mining. Data mining is an important part of data science, without it there's no data for data scientists to work on. A lot of data scientists spend a large amount of time extracting, cleaning, and transforming data.

Data can be mined from different sources. The internet is full of data, structured or unstructured. It takes a while to gather unstructured data due to their lack of order while structured data are easier to find and analyze because they are organized. Examples of unstructured data include emails, images, audio, videos, pdfs, and posts on social media. Structured data includes data that is organized and separated into different categories such as age, name, date, gender, address, length, breadth, width, etc.

Most data scientists work on structured data since it's easier to find and analyze. The major sources of structured data include spreadsheets, SQL databases, online forms, sensors, medical devices, and web pages.

How to Extract Data from a File

Data that exist in a file can be accessed and read by the interpreter through the following instructions:

```python
read_file = open( 'Data_file.txt', 'r' )
# 'r' directs the interpreter to only read the
file
read_lines = read_lines.readlines() #  this  will
read the lines in the text line by line #
write_file = open( 'Science.txt', 'w' )
# 'w' will create a new file named Science if it
does not exist in the Lib directory! and destroy
any existing file
append_file = open('appending_file.txt', 'a' )
# 'a' will append or add to the bottom of the
existing file

write_file.close()
# this will close the file
```

It's quite common for programmers to forget to close a file after they are done with coding, to prevent this the open statement is written with a with block.

```python
with  open( read_file.txt, 'r' ) as f:
data1 = read( f )
```

When the with block is done, the file closes.

How to Extract Text from Web Pages

Most web pages are written in HTML, the text separated into different categories and characteristics/ tags.

```html
<html> site address
   <head> name of site
      <title> name of article</title>
   </head> heading of article
   <body>  body of article
         <p id="author">name of writer</p>
```

```
    <p id="subject">topic</p>
  </body>
</html>
```

However, not all HTML are written in such an organized format. If they were, it would be so much easier to extract text from them by writing a simple program that finds the 'paragraph' element whose identifier is 'id' and prints what it contains. Once the HTML isn't written in an organized format, you will need additional help to make sense of it and extract data from it. This help will come in the form of a library called Beautiful Soup. It creates a tree for the elements on the webpage, increasing the accessibility. The latest update is the Beautiful Soup 4.8.0. You can find the statement to download it at this website. If this is your first time installing a library, you'll find that it's not difficult once you have a clear idea of what to do.

How to Install a Library

1. Open the command prompt on your system. There are different ways to do this, it depends on your operating system.

   - For Windows, open the search tab and type 'cmd' which is an acronym for command prompt. Click on it.

   - For Linux, press Ctrl + Alt + T your the keyboard. It will immediately bring up the terminal. Another method is to press the windows button and type 'terminal'. The command prompt is known as terminal in Linux and Mac.

- For Mac, open the applications file, click on the utilities folder and double click the Terminal file. An alternate method is to press Command + Space, it will open the Spotlight tab. Type terminal and double click the result of the search.

2. Once the command prompt is open, type the install instruction found on the library's website and press enter.

3. Wait for it to download, then you're ready.

4. Once installed, you import the library into Python with the import keyword.

To install Beautiful Soup, the install statement is `pip install beautifulsoup4`. The Requests library is needed as it has a much nicer way of requesting HTTPs than the method built into Python. A more tolerant parser is also needed. Python's in-built parser is not so forgiving to websites with HTML's that are not well organized. To install the necessary parser type `pip install html5lib` in the command prompt. For Requests, the install statement is `pip install requests`.

To use the three libraries imported, the statement is structured as:

```
from bs4    import        BeautifulSoup
import         requests
html  =        requests.get(
"http://www.website.com" ).text
# the parenthesis holds the site that contains
the data
soup  =        BeautifulSoup(html,      'html5lib')
```

Once that is done, you can get the text and contents of the site by :

```python
Paragraph_1 = soup.p     #to find the first <p>
element
Paragraph_1_text = soup.p.text
Paragraph_1_words = soup.p.text.split( )
```

You can also extract it's characteristics by treating the tags like a dictionary

```python
Paragraph_1_id1 = soup.p['id']       #  causes  a
KeyError if there is no 'id'
Paragraph_1_id2 = soup.p.get('id') # alternative
method, does not raise a keyerror, just prints
none.
```

You can extract multiple tags at once with:

```python
Paragraph_all  =  soup.find_all('p') # or  just
soup('p')
All_paragraphs_with_ids = [p for p in soup( 'p'
) if p.get('id')]
```

To get tags with specific class:

```python
Main_paragraphs = soup( 'p', { 'class' : 'main'
} )
Main_paragraphs2 = soup( 'p', 'main' )
Main_paragraphs3 = [p for p in soup('p')
            if 'main' in p.get('class',  [ ] ) ]
```

You can merge these formats to get a more specific data. To find every <small> tag in the <section> tags, type

```python
smalls_inside_section = [ span
    for div in soup( 'section' )
# for each <section> on the page
    for small in section( 'small' ) ]
# find each <small> in <section>
```

NB: For full understanding of HTML and its tags, visit website.

This handful of features of a site will allow you to do a lot, however, you won't be able to get some complicated data this way. Not all main data or content will be labelled main, in most cases, you will have to inspect (ctrl + shift+ I on Windows) the webpage.

How to Scrape Data from a Website

This will involve a combinate of all you've learned so far.

NB: JSON is an acronym for JavaScript Object Notation. It is used to transport and store data from webpages.

Example 1.

1. The site to scrape is www.amazon.com.

2. The mission is to build a program that extracts the following details from the site

    - Name of the product

    - Category

    - List Price

    - Deal Price

    - Availability

    - URL of the product.

3. The problems the program solves

    - Extract product details that can't be acquired with Product Advertising API: Amazon designed a

Product Advertising API for users, but like most website's API, it does not produce all the info Amazon gives on a product page. *The program must be able to extract all the details shown on a product page.*

- Monitor changes in the price of products , availability, and rating: *The program must be designed to monitor the products. .*

4. The required packages to build the program

- Python 2.7

- pip

- Requests library

- Lxml library (website)

The Code

The first thing to do is to inspect the site if it permits data scraping. To do that, go to the terms and conditions of the site. Amazon permits extraction of data as long as it's used to add value to the world. Another method is to check the robots.txt file of the site. This is done by adding robots.txt to the end of the sites' URL.

www.amazon.com/robots.txt

The program is designed to extract details of some sneakers sold on Amazon:

```
from lxml import html
import csv,os,json
import requests
```

```python
from exceptions import ValueError
from time import sleep

def AmazonProductParser(url):
    heading = {'User-Agent': 'Mozilla/5.0 (X11;
Linux x86_64) AppleWebKit/537.36 (KHTML, like
Gecko) Chrome/42.0.2311.90 Safari/537.36'}
    page = requests.get(url,heading=heading)
    while True:
        sleep(3)
        try:
            doc = html.fromstring(page.content)
            XPATH_NAME =
'//h1[@id="title"]//text()'
            XPATH_DEAL_PRICE =
'//span[contains(@id,"ourprice") or
contains(@id,"saleprice")]/text()'
            XPATH_REAL_PRICE =
'//td[contains(text(),"List Price") or
contains(text(),"M.R.P") or
contains(text(),"Price")]/following-
sibling::td/text()'
            XPATH_CATEGORY = '//a[@class="a-
link-normal a-color-tertiary"]//text()'
            XPATH_STOCK_AVAILABILITY =
'//div[@id="availability"]//text()'

            PRODUCT_NAME = doc.xpath(XPATH_NAME)
            PRODUCT_DEAL_PRICE =
doc.xpath(XPATH_DEAL_PRICE)
            PRODUCT_CATEGORY =
doc.xpath(XPATH_CATEGORY)
            PRODUCT_REAL_PRICE =
doc.xpath(XPATH_REAL_PRICE)
```

```python
        PRODUCT_STOCK_AVAILABILITY =
doc.xpath(XPATH_STOCK_AVAILABILITY)

        NAME = ' '.join(''.join(
PRODUCT_NAME).split()) if PRODUCT_NAME else None
        DEAL_PRICE = ' '.join(''.join(
PRODUCT_DEAL_PRICE).split()).strip() if
PRODUCT_DEAL_PRICE else None
        CATEGORY = ' > '.join([i.strip() for
i in PRODUCT_CATEGORY]) if PRODUCT_CATEGORY else
None
        REAL_PRICE = ''.join(
PRODUCT_REAL_PRICE).strip() if
PRODUCT_REAL_PRICE else None
        AVAILABILITY = ''.join(
PRODUCT_STOCK_AVAILABILITY).strip() if
PRODUCT_STOCK_AVAILABILITY else None

        if not REAL_PRICE:
            REAL_PRICE = DEAL_PRICE

        if page.status_code!=200:
            raise ValueError('captha')
        data = {
                'NAME':NAME,
                'DEAL_PRICE':DEAL_PRICE,
                'CATEGORY':CATEGORY,
                'REAL_PRICE':REAL_PRICE,

'STOCK_AVAILABILITY':AVAILABILITY,
                'URL':url,
                }

        return data
    except Exception as e:
```

```python
        print (e)

def ReadAsin():              #ASIN is the sneaker's
product identification number
    # AsinList =
csv.DictReader(open(os.path.join(os.path.dirname
(__file__),"Asinfeed.csv")))
    AsinList = ['B07KC21BMT', 'B07DPRQMDH',
'B07DPSVJMN', 'B07417N22S', 'B073Y6MPR3',
'B0711R2TNB', 'B000ARG5T8', 'B00D881KE6',
'B07TWMDM6Z', 'B07FYB1H5J',]
    extracted_data = []
    for i in AsinList:
        url = "http://www.amazon.com/dp/"+i
        print ("Processing: "+url)

extracted_data.append(AmazonProductParser(url))
        sleep(5)
    f = open(' Sneakers.json','w')
    json.dump(extracted_data,f,indent=4)
    print (" Done Scrapping Amazon Sneakers.
Check the data file in directory ")

if __name__ == "__main__":
    ReadAsin()
```

The output of the program:

```
Processing: http://www.amazon.com/dp/B07KC21BMT
Processing: http://www.amazon.com/dp/B07DPRQMDH
Processing: http://www.amazon.com/dp/B07DPSVJMN
Processing: http://www.amazon.com/dp/B07417N22S
Processing: http://www.amazon.com/dp/B073Y6MPR3
Processing: http://www.amazon.com/dp/B0711R2TNB
Processing: http://www.amazon.com/dp/B000ARG5T8
```

```
Processing: http://www.amazon.com/dp/B00D881KE6
Processing: http://www.amazon.com/dp/B07TWMDM6Z
Processing: http://www.amazon.com/dp/B07FYB1H5J
Done Scrapping Amazon Sneakers. Check the data
file in directory
```

The data file will be named Sneakers and it will be a .json file. It can be opened with MS Word. The data in the file will have the following structure

```
{
        "NAME":  "Teva   Lightweight   Waterproof
Comfort  Hiking  Training  Boxing  Wrestling  Gym
Arrowood Swift Mid Premier Sneakers",
        "DEAL_PRICE": "$49.99 - $57.98",
        "CATEGORY": "Clothing, Shoes & Jewelry >
Men > Shoes > Fashion Sneakers",
        "REAL_PRICE": "$49.99 - $57.98",
        "STOCK_AVAILABILITY": null,
        "URL":
"http://www.amazon.com/dp/B073Y6MPR3"
    },
    {
        "NAME":  "adidas  Women's  Cloudfoam  Pure
Running Shoe",
        "DEAL_PRICE":  "$35.00  -  $155.00  Lower
price available on select options",
        "CATEGORY": "Clothing, Shoes & Jewelry >
Women > Shoes > Fashion Sneakers",
        "REAL_PRICE":  "$35.00  -  $155.00  Lower
price available on select options",
        "STOCK_AVAILABILITY": null,
        "URL":
"http://www.amazon.com/dp/B0711R2TNB"
    },
```

That is the details of 2 of the 10 sneakers present in the program. The remaining details can be found in the Sneakers file.

Mission Successful! You've created a program that extracts the product details from Amazon.

Program 2.

1. The site to mine is www.amazon.com.

2. The mission is to build a program that extracts the reviews of some products on the site

3. The program can be used to

    - To perform data analysis with the reviews as the source of data

    - Create a database of Amazon reviews.

5. The required packages to build the program

    - Python 3.0

    - pip

    - Requests library

    - Lxml library (website)

    - Dateutil (website)

The Code

After inspecting the site for permissions, create the program:

```python
# -*- coding: utf-8 -*- #       this       help       the
interpreter deal with the Unicode characters in
the product details
from lxml import html
from json import dump, loads
from requests import get
import json
from re import sub
from dateutil import parser as dateparser
from time import sleep
def ExtractReviews(asin):

    amzon_url =
'http://www.amazon.com/dp/'+asin
    heading = {'User-Agent': 'Mozilla/5.0 (X11;
Linux x86_64) AppleWebKit/537.36 (KHTML, like
Gecko) Chrome/62.0.3202.94 Safari/537.36'}
    for i in range(5):
        reply = get(amzon_url, heading =
heading, verify=False, timeout=30)
        if reply.status_code == 404:
            return {"url": amzon_url, "error":
"page not found"}
        if reply.status_code != 200:
            continue

        # Removing the null bytes from the
reply.
        clean_reply = reply.text.replace('\x00',
'')

        parser_ = html.fromstring(clean_reply)
```

```python
        XPATH_AGGREGATE_ =
'//span[@id="acrCustomerReviewText"]'
        XPATH_REVIEW_SECTION_1_ =
'//div[contains(@id,"reviews-summary")]'
        XPATH_REVIEW_SECTION_2_ = '//div[@data-
hook="review"]'
        XPATH_AGGREGATE__RATING_ =
'//table[@id="histogramTable"]//tr'
        XPATH_PRODUCT_NAME_=
'//h1//span[@id="productTitle"]//text()'
        XPATH_PRODUCT_PRICE_ =
'//span[@id="priceblock_ourprice"]/text()'
        raw_product_price =
parser_.xpath(XPATH_PRODUCT_PRICE_)
        raw_product_name =
parser_.xpath(XPATH_PRODUCT_NAME_)
        total_ratings  =
parser_.xpath(XPATH_AGGREGATE__RATING_)
        reviews =
parser_.xpath(XPATH_REVIEW_SECTION_1_)
        product_price =
''.join(raw_product_price).replace(',', '')
        product_name =
''.join(raw_product_name).strip()
        if not reviews:
            reviews =
parser_.xpath(XPATH_REVIEW_SECTION_2_)
        ratings_dict = {}
        reviews_list = []
        # Grabing the rating section in product
page
        for ratings in total_ratings:
            extracted_rating =
ratings.xpath('./td//a//text()')
            if extracted_rating:
```

```python
                rating_key = extracted_rating[0]
                raw_raing_value =
extracted_rating[1]
                rating_value = raw_raing_value
                if rating_key:

ratings_dict.update({rating_key: rating_value})


        # extracting individual reviews
        for review in reviews:
            XPATH_RATING_  = './/i[@data-
hook="review-star-rating"]//text()'
            XPATH_REVIEW_HEADER = './/a[@data-
hook="review-title"]//text()'
            XPATH_REVIEW_POSTED_DATE =
'.//span[@data-hook="review-date"]//text()'
            XPATH_REVIEW_TEXT_1 = './/div[@data-
hook="review-collapsed"]//text()'
            XPATH_REVIEW_TEXT_2 =
'.//div//span[@data-action="columnbalancing-
showfullreview"]/@data-columnbalancing-
showfullreview'
            XPATH_REVIEW_COMMENTS =
'.//span[@data-hook="review-comment"]//text()'
            XPATH_AUTHOR =
'.//span[contains(@class,"profile-
name")]//text()'
            XPATH_REVIEW_TEXT_3 =
'.//div[contains(@id,"dpReviews")]/div/text()'

            raw_review_author =
review.xpath(XPATH_AUTHOR)
            raw_review_rating =
review.xpath(XPATH_RATING_)
```

```python
                raw_review_header =
review.xpath(XPATH_REVIEW_HEADER)
                raw_review_posted_date =
review.xpath(XPATH_REVIEW_POSTED_DATE)
                raw_review_text1 =
review.xpath(XPATH_REVIEW_TEXT_1)
                raw_review_text2 =
review.xpath(XPATH_REVIEW_TEXT_2)
                raw_review_text3 =
review.xpath(XPATH_REVIEW_TEXT_3)
                # Cleaning data
                author = ' '.join('
'.join(raw_review_author).split())
                review_rating =
''.join(raw_review_rating).replace('out of 5
stars', '')
                review_header = ' '.join('
'.join(raw_review_header).split())
                try:
                    review_posted_date =
dateparser_.parse(''.join(raw_review_posted_date
)).strftime('%d %b %Y')
                except:
                    review_posted_date = None
                review_text = ' '.join('
'.join(raw_review_text1).split())
                # Grabbing hidden comments if
present
                if raw_review_text2:
                    json_loaded_review_data =
loads(raw_review_text2[0])
                    json_loaded_review_data_text =
json_loaded_review_data['rest']

cleaned_json_loaded_review_data_text =
```

```python
                re.sub('<.*?>', '',
json_loaded_review_data_text)
                    full_review_text =
review_text+cleaned_json_loaded_review_data_text
                else:
                    full_review_text = review_text
                if not raw_review_text1:
                    full_review_text = ' '.join('
'.join(raw_review_text3).split())
                raw_review_comments =
review.xpath(XPATH_REVIEW_COMMENTS)
                review_comments =
''.join(raw_review_comments)
                review_comments = sub('[A-Za-z]',
'', review_comments).strip()
                review_dict = {

'review_comment_count': review_comments,
                                    'review_text':
full_review_text,

'review_posted_date': review_posted_date,
                                    'review_header':
review_header,
                                    'review_rating':
review_rating,
                                    'review_author':
author
                                }
                reviews_list.append(review_dict)
            data = {
                        'ratings': ratings_dict,
                        'reviews': reviews_list,
                        'url': amzon_url,
                        'name': product_name,
```

```python
                    'price': product_price

                }
        return data
    return { "error": "failed to process the
page", "url": amzon_url }

def ReadAsin():
    # Add your own ASINs here
    AsinList = [ 'B07KC21BMT',
    'B07DPRQMDH',
    'B07DPSVJMN',
    'B07417N22S',
    'B073Y6MPR3',
    'B0711R2TNB',
    'B000ARG5T8',
    'B00D881KE6',
    'B07TWMDM6Z',
    'B07FYB1H5J', ]
    extracted_data = []

    for asin in AsinList:
        print ( "Downloading and processing page
http://www.amazon.com/dp/" + asin )

extracted_data.append(ExtractReviews(asin))
        sleep(5)
    f = open('Sneaker reviews.json', 'w')
    dump(extracted_data, f, indent=4)
    f.close()
    print ( " Done Scrapping Amazon Sneakers.
Check the data file in directory. " )
if __name__ == '__main__':
    ReadAsin()
```

The interpreter will run the program and print in the window:

```
Downloading and processing page
http://www.amazon.com/dp/B07KC21BMT
Downloading and processing page
http://www.amazon.com/dp/B07DPRQMDH
Downloading and processing page
http://www.amazon.com/dp/B07DPSVJMN
Downloading and processing page
http://www.amazon.com/dp/B073Y6MPR3
Downloading and processing page
http://www.amazon.com/dp/B0711R2TNB
Downloading and processing page
http://www.amazon.com/dp/B000ARG5T8
Downloading and processing page
http://www.amazon.com/dp/B00D881KE6
Downloading and processing page
http://www.amazon.com/dp/B07TWMDM6Z
Downloading and processing page
http://www.amazon.com/dp/B07FYB1H5J
Done Scrapping Amazon Sneakers. Check the data
file in the directory.
```

The data file is present in a 'sneaker reviews.json file'. The file will contain:

```
[
    {
        "ratings": {
            "5 star": "60%",
            "4 star": "19%",
            "3 star": "6%",
            "2 star": "5%",
            "1 star": "10%"
        },
```

        "reviews": [
            {
                "review_comment_count": "",
                "review_text": "They so white ,
my shoes voted for trump. They so white I got
pulled over and the cop kept on going . They so
white my credit scored jumped They so white I
started balancing my checkbook They so white I
took some random kids to soccer practice and
gave them orange slices They so white I started
singing the national.... Now my knees dirty",
                "review_posted_date": "19 Oct
2018",
                "review_header": "You can wear
em to bed",
                "review_rating": "5.0 ",
                "review_author": "Tony"
            },
            {
                "review_comment_count": "",
                "review_text": "I love em! Looks
good ..fits great..thanks you to who ever
created this shoe ..its clean and casual ..im
getting every color.",
                "review_posted_date": "11 Jul
2018",
                "review_header": "I love em!
Looks good",
                "review_rating": "5.0 ",
                "review_author": "Preston Moore"
            },
            {
                "review_comment_count": "",
                "review_text": "Love them!
Pretty comfortable and breathable shoes. Looks

just like in the photos! I really like wearing
them & they are just what I was looking for.
Great seller, communicates and very fast
shipping five stars. Definitely buying again.",
                "review_posted_date": "27 Jul
2018",
                "review_header": "Love them!
It\u2019s worth it buy them!!!",
                "review_rating": "5.0 ",
                "review_author": "Gabby
Lavorata"
            },
            {
                "review_comment_count": "",
                "review_text": "I\u2019m not a
name brand person so them being knock offs
didn\u2019t bother me. I wore them to a concert
and to a park they are very comfortable",
                "review_posted_date": "10 Oct
2018",
                "review_header": "Comfortable",
                "review_rating": "5.0 ",
                "review_author": "Anonymous"
            },
            {
                "review_comment_count": "",
                "review_text": "Fit true to
size. Good quality for the money. Expected alot
less. Was very comfortable. Shoelaces more for
show than to actually use. material is a
stretchy mesh knit. It's very lightweight.",
                "review_posted_date": "05 Jul
2018",
                "review_header": "Cant beat for
the price!",

            "review_rating": "5.0 ",
            "review_author": "becca bodey"
        },
        {
            "review_comment_count": "",
            "review_text": "Not bad at all!
I really like them for the house and running
quick errands. soft, gentle, stylish. I
recommend to size down.",
            "review_posted_date": "30 Oct
2018",
            "review_header": "Impressive!",
            "review_rating": "5.0 ",
            "review_author": "tania mattos"
        },
        {
            "review_comment_count": "",
            "review_text": "They fit perfect
for me.I would recommend them to anyone.
Especially since I have special made devices on
my feet & legs Thank you",
            "review_posted_date": "04 Aug
2018",
            "review_header": "AWESOME
SHOES!!!",
            "review_rating": "5.0 ",
            "review_author": "Country Girl"
        },
        {
            "review_comment_count": "",
            "review_text": "They are so
breathable and comfortable and very beatiful, I
cant wait to wear them to join the party.",
            "review_posted_date": "13 Oct
2018",

```
                "review_header": "breathable
comfortable beautiful",
                "review_rating": "5.0 ",
                "review_author": "arthas"
        }
    ],
```

This is the review of 1 of the sneakers listed in the program. The other reviews can be found in the .json file.

There are many more sites to scrape information and extract data from. Twitter, Facebook, MySpace, and various other social media platforms are good sources of data. Like Amazon, you can access the data on the sites through their API. They all have libraries created a to allow programmers to interact with the API's e.g Twython for Twitter.

Chapter 10

Data Visualization

The creation and analysis of the visual depiction of data is known as data visualization. It involves the use of information graphics, graph plots, statistical graphics and various other tools to represent data and communicate it's information effectively. Data visualization is art and it's also science, it's an incredible combination of both to produce an image that clearly expresses the information in the data. It helps to present data in a manner that easy to interpret by almost anyone.

Learning how to represent data visually is a fundamental part of a data scientist's job. While it's easy to create visuals on paper, it's rather difficult to make good ones on Python. Don't get scared! With the right tools in place, visualizing data with Python can also be easy. One of such tools is the 'matplotlib' library. It can be used to create simple bar charts, scatter plots, and line charts. Other libraries include seaborn, D3.js (used for Java), Bokeh, and ggplot. Matplotlib might be the oldest of the libraries listed but it's the easiest to use. It can achieve both simple and complicated visualizations.

How to use Matplotlib to Create a Simple Line Chart

Download the library with the install statement found on the website. Import the pyplot module from the library. The module allows you to build your visualization one step at a time. It can be done with the command statement:

```
from matplotlib import pyplot as plt
```

After adding the details of the data to a list, the details of the graph is specified with the plt. function. The resulting visual representation is be saved with plt.savefig( ) and displayed with plt.show( ).

Example

A local basketball club requested a visual representation of how their fans grew over the years. Construct a line chart with the data recorded by the club.

Year	1988	1992	1996	2000	2004	2008	2012	2016
Fans	32	46	75	150	173	250	295	380

Solution:

```
#program that demonstrates how to construct a
simple line chart
from matplotlib import pyplot as plt
year = [ 1988,1992, 1996, 2000, 2004, 2008,
2012, 2016 ] #list 1
fans = [32, 46, 75, 150, 173, 250, 295, 380]

plt.plot(year, fans , color = 'blue', marker =
'*', linestyle = 'dotted')
# the first item in the parentheses specifies
the list on the x axis ( years )
```

```python
# the second item in the parentheses specifies
the list on the y-axis ( fans )
# the third item in the parentheses specifies
colour of the line
# the fourth item in the parentheses specifies
the shape of each point on the line
# the fifth item in the parentheses specifies
the style of the line
plt.title( " Growth of Fans from 1988 to 2016 "
)      #title of line chart
plt.ylabel( " Fans " )  # labels the y axis
plt.xlabel( " Years " )        #labels the x axis
plt.show( )
plt.savefig( )
```

The output of the program:

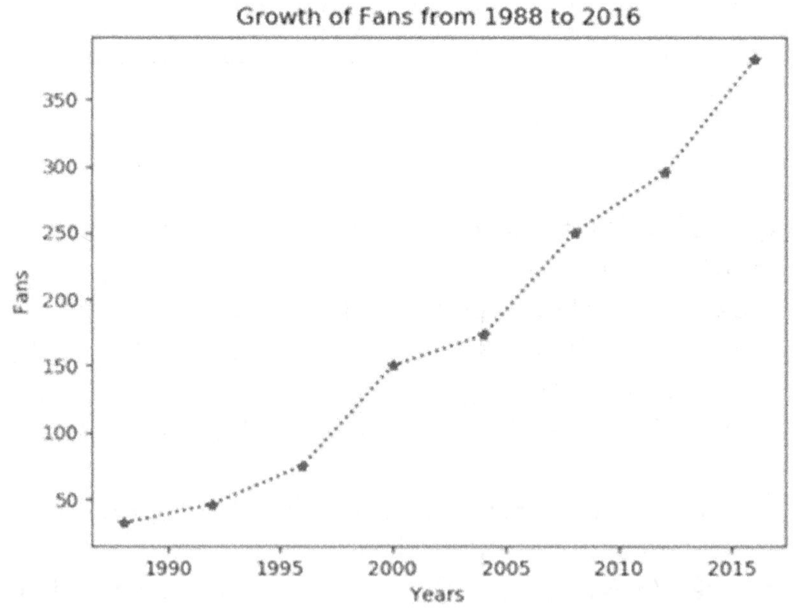

NB:

- The color of the line can be specified as any of the 7 main colours.

- The marker can be specified as +, o, and *

- The style of the line can be specified as '-', '--', '-.', ':', 'None', ' ', '', 'solid', 'dashed', 'dashdot', and 'dotted'.

How to use Matplotlib to Create a Simple Bar Chart

The statements used to create a bar chart with matplotlib is identical to those of line charts, with a little modifications here and there. plt.plot is used for line chart while plt.bar is used for bar chart.

Example

A local basketball club requested a visual representation of how their fans grew over the years. Construct a bar chart with the data recorded by the club.

Year	1988	1992	1996	2000	2004	2008	2012	2016
Fans	32	46	150	75	250	173	173	380

Solution:

```
#program that demonstrates how to construct a
simple bar chart
from matplotlib import pyplot as plt
year = [ 1988,1992, 1996, 2000, 2004, 2008,
2012, 2016 ] #list 1
fans = [32, 46, 150, 75, 250, 173, 173, 380]
```

```python
year_w = [ i + 0.15 for i, _ in enumerate( year
) ]

#default width of the bar is 0.8, the statement
above adds 0.15 to the width
plt.bar(year_w, fans )  # plot bars with left x-
coordinates [ year_w ] and heights  [ fans ]
plt.title( " Bar chart of Fans Every Four Years
" )   #title of bar chart
plt.ylabel( " Fans " )  # labels the y axis
plt.xticks ( [ i + 0.1 for i, _ in enumerate(
year )], year )
#labels the bars according to their respective
years
plt.show( )
plt.savefig( )
```

The output of the program above:

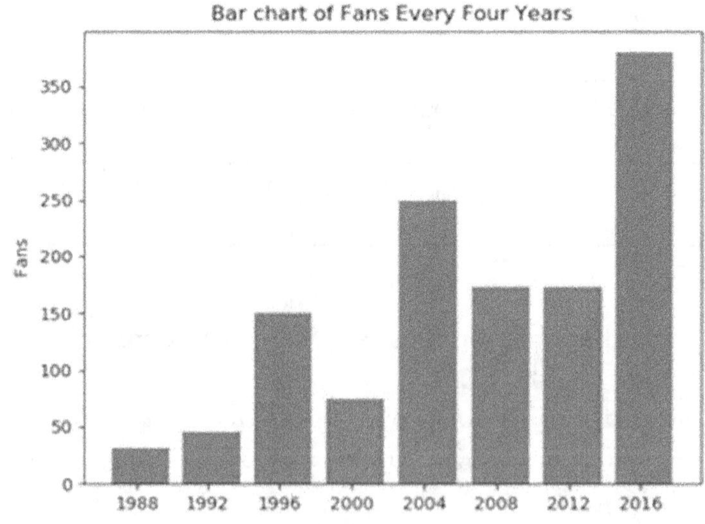

The statements used to create a bar chart can be modified to produce a histogram. There is a need to modify the width of the bars and adjust the x axis to become suitable for a histogram. Practice this.

How to use Matplotlib to Create Scatterplots

A scatterplot is arguably the best choice for visualizing a relationship between a paired set of data. plt.scatter statement is used to instruct the interpreter to create a scatterplot.

Example

A local basketball club requested a visual representation of how their fans grew over the years. Construct a scatterplot with the data recorded by the club.

S/N	1	2	3	4	5	6	7	8
Year	1988	1992	1996	2000	2004	2008	2012	2016
Fans	32	46	150	75	250	173	173	380

Solution:

```
#program that demonstrates how to construct a
scatterplot
from matplotlib import pyplot as plt
year = [ 1988,1992, 1996, 2000, 2004, 2008,
2012, 2016 ]
fans = [ 32, 46, 150, 75, 250, 173, 173, 380 ]
year_number = [ 1, 2, 3, 4, 5, 6, 7, 8  ]
plt.scatter( year, fans )
```

```python
for year_number, year_count, fan_count in zip(
year_number, year, fans ):
    #label each point in the graph
    plt.annotate(year_number,
        xy=(year_count, fan_count),

        xytext = (4,     -4), #       but
    slightly    offset
        textcoords ='offset    points')

plt.title( " Fan base vs Year " )
plt.ylabel( " Fans " )
plt.xlabel ( "Years" )
plt.show( )
plt.savefig( )
```

The output of the program:

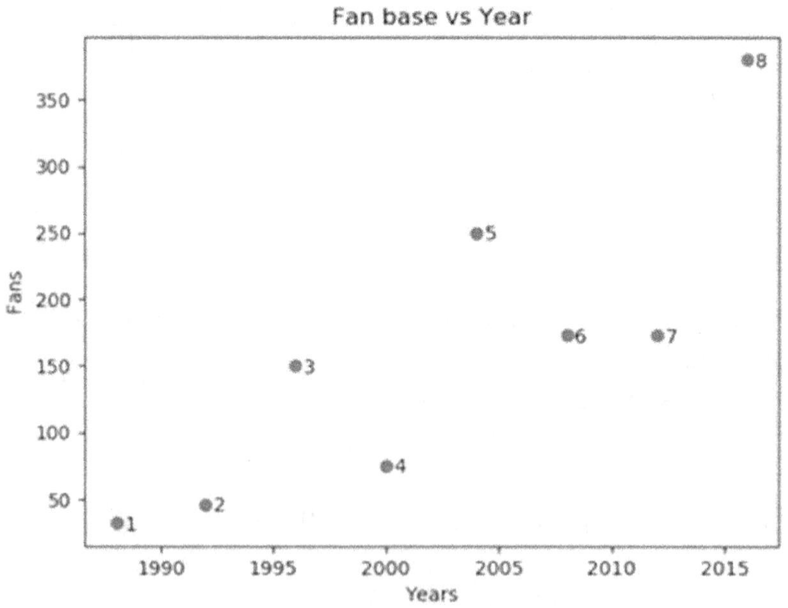

This program is suitable for data that is not comparing variables of the same type. To compare two similar variables, the interpreter must be instructed to start the axis at the same point with the plt.axis statement.

Example

A test was carried out in two classes, A and B. There are 10 high school students in class A and 10 middle school students in class B. Each student was given a number from 1 to 10, construct a scatterplot graph that compares the results of their grades according to their number.

S/N	1	2	3	4	5	6	7	8	9	10
Class A	8	20	48	55	67	74	81	89	92	97
Class B	32	47	49	50	63	73	80	80	98	99

Solution:

```python
#program that demonstrates how to construct a
scatterplot with equal axis
from matplotlib import pyplot as plt
Class_A = [ 8, 20, 48, 55, 67, 74, 81, 89, 92,
95 ]
Class_B = [ 32, 47, 49, 50, 63, 73, 80, 80, 88,
99 ]

Student_number = [ 1, 2, 3, 4, 5, 6, 7, 8, 9, 10
]
plt.scatter( Class_A, Class_B )
for Student_number, A_count, B_count in zip(
Student_number, Class_A, Class_B ):
```

```python
plt.annotate( Student_number,
    xy=( A_count,    B_count),
    xytext = (5,      -5),
    textcoords ='offset    points')

plt.title( " High School vs Middle School " )
plt.axis([ 0,100, 0, 100 ] )          # specify the
beginning and the ending of each axis
plt.ylabel( " Middle School " )
plt.xlabel ( " High School " )
plt.show( )
plt.savefig( )
```

Output:

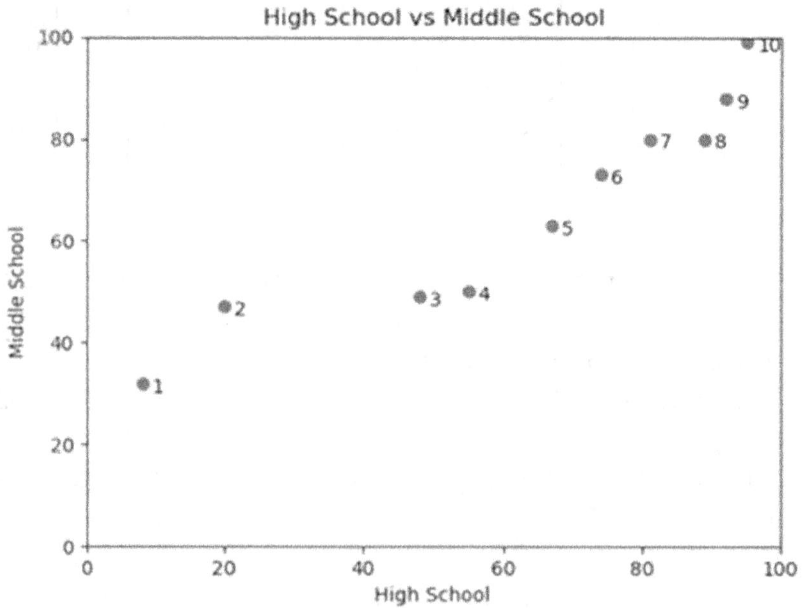

Matplotlib is not only limited to line charts, bar charts, and scatterplots, it can be used for various other graph illustrations such as:

- Paths

- Three-dimensional plotting

- Streamplot

- Pie charts

- Tables

- Filled curves

- Log plots

- Polar plots, and many more.

Chapter 11

Linear Algebra

Algebra originated from the Arabic word 'al-jabr' meaning "the reunion of broken parts". It involves the use of known parts to find out unknown parts in mathematics. Linear Algebra is a branch of algebra that is concerned with linear functions and linear equations. Basically, it is used to explain geometric terms like planes in different dimensions and allows the performance of mathematical calculations on them (planes). Ordinarily, algebra focuses on one-dimensional scalar while linear algebra deals multi-dimensional vectors and matrices.

Previous knowledge of linear algebra is not necessarily a prerequisite for data science, however, you will need to master some aspects of the topic that are absolutely necessary in data science. There are four ways in which linear algebra is used in data science

- Scalar

- Vectors

- Matrix

- Tensor

Scalars are simple numbers. Vectors are one-dimensional array, lists in Python, used for storing data. Vectors are an excellent way to store numeric data. Multiple vectors can be joined together to form a new vector, multiplication by scalars also results in new vectors. For example, if you have to store the details of a large amount of people, you can convert the details into multi-dimensional vectors.

Example

1. During the health week, a company collected the health information of all the workers in a company. The human resources department had to record the age, weight, and heights of all workers. Convert the details for each worker into a three-dimensional vector.

S/N	1	2	3	4	5	6	7	8	9	10
Age	32	26	45	54	27	21	28	23	26	30
Weight (kg)	81	61	74	72	75	65	80	68	78	83
Height (cm)	164	165	171	170	179	177	187	155	180	185

Solution:

```
from numpy import array          # used to create
arrays in python
Worker1 = array( [ 32,           # age
              81,                # weight,
              164 ] )            # height
Worker2 = array( [ 26,
              61,
              165 ] )
Worker3 = array( [ 45,
              74,
              171 ] )
Worker4 = array( [ 54,
```

$$72,$$
$$170]) \ldots$$

The list can go on and on. Mathematical calculations can be performed with the data in the vector as long as the vectors are of equal length i.e have the same number of elements. It's not possible to add a two dimensional vector to a three dimensional vector. To find the sum of the ages, weight, and height of two of the workers in the company:

```python
from numpy import array
def vector_add( a, b ):
    y = a + b
    print ( y )
    return
Worker2 = array( [ 26,
                   61,
                   165 ] )
Worker3 = array( [ 45,
                   74,
                   171 ] )
vector_add( Worker2, Worker3)
```

Output of the program:

```
[ 71   135    336]
```

2. Grade 5 students in a school wrote 5 exams each on different topics. The exams were graded over 50, however, the results of the exam need to be recorded over a hundred. Create a five-dimensional vector with the grades and convert the scores over a hundred.

S/N	Maths	English	Geography	Spanish	Science
1	37	42	37	23	39
2	45	41	48	36	47
3	32	39	21	15	21
4	35	38	33	36	35
5	22	48	37	34	26

Solution:

```python
from numpy import array
def vector_multiply( a, c ):
y = c*a
        print ( y )
        return
Maths = array( [ 37,
                 45,
                 32,
                 35,
                 22 ] )
English = array( [ 42,
                 41,
                 39,
                 38,
                 48 ] )
Geography = array( [ 37,
                 48,
                 21,
                 33,
                 37 ] )
Spanish = array( [ 23,
                 36,
                 15,
```

```
                        36,
                        34 ] )
        Science = array( [ 39,
                        47,
                        21,
                        35,
                        26 ] )
        print (" The score over hundred in Maths: ")
        vector_multiply( Maths, 2)
        print (" The score over hundred in English: ")
        vector_multiply( English, 2)
        print (" The score over hundred in Geography: ")
        vector_multiply( Geography, 2)
        print (" The score over hundred in Spanish: ")
        vector_multiply( Spanish, 2)
        print (" The score over hundred in Science: ")
        vector_multiply( Science, 2)
```

Output:

```
The score over hundred in Maths:
[74 90 64 70 44]
 The score over hundred in English:
[84 82 78 76 96]
 The score over hundred in Geography:
[74 96 42 66 74]
 The score over hundred in Spanish:
[46 72 30 72 68]
 The score over hundred in Science:
[78 94 42 70 52]
```

All other mathematical operations on vectors follows this principles. Matrices are two-dimensional arrays used to store numbers. They are popularly known as the lists of lists, with each lists having the same number of rows and columns. If M is a matrix, M[a] [b] is interpreted as an element in the ath row and b^{th} column. Capital letters are typically used to represent matrices. For example,

```
G = [[ 37, 45, 32, 35, 22],    # matrix G has 5
                               rows and 5 columns.
    [ 42, 41, 39, 38, 48],      # row 1 represents
                               English grades
    [ 37, 48, 21, 33, 37],      # row 2 represents
                               Geography grades
    [ 23, 36, 15, 36, 34],      # row 3 represents
                               Spanish grades
    [ 39,   47, 21, 35, 26] ]   # row 4 represents
                               Science grades
```

Remember that python starts counting from zero, so row 1 contains the grades of the students that participated in the exam. To access the Spanish grade of second student, the correct representation is G[3] [1].

```
>>>    print G[ 3 ] [ 1 ]
       36
```

A matrix with a rows and b columns is referred to as an "a **X** b" matrix. The row and column of the matrix can also be thought of as a vector of length b and length a respectively. Matrices are important in data science to represent data with multiple vectors, the same way the individual five-dimensional vectors of the exam grades was converted to a single matrix.

Matrix is an excellent way of expressing a binary relationship in Python. This means that it can be used to find out the relationship between two entities.

Example

There are 100 students in a class, 36 are female and the rest are male. The students are divided into ten groups with each student getting a number from one to ten. The females are assigned an additional means of identification, the number 1, while the males were assigned the number 0. Represent this data in a matrix.

Solution:

```
S =   [ [0, 1, 0, 0, 0, 1, 0, 0, 1, 0 ],   # group 1
                                            row 0
      [0, 0, 1, 0, 0, 0, 1, 0, 0, 1 ],
      [0, 1, 1, 0, 0, 1, 1, 0, 0, 0 ],
      [0, 0, 1, 0, 1, 0, 0, 1, 0, 0 ],
      [0, 0, 0, 0, 0, 0, 0, 0, 0, 0 ],
      [0, 1, 0, 0, 1, 0, 1, 0, 0, 1 ],
      [0, 1, 0, 1, 0, 0, 1, 1, 1, 0 ],
      [1, 0, 1, 0, 1, 0, 1, 0, 0, 0 ],
      [1, 1, 0, 0, 1, 1, 0, 0, 1, 0 ],
      [1, 1, 0, 1, 0, 0, 0, 0, 1, 1 ] ]
```

If a number is chosen at random, it's quite easy to find out if the the student with the corresponding number is male or female.

```
if S[ 5 ][ 8 ] == 1:
    print ( ' Female ' )
else:
    print ( " Male " )
```

The output of the program after execution:

```
Male
```

The number chosen belongs to a male student. Matrices make it easy
to find connections within elements in a list. To find out if two
random numbers are of the same gender:

```python
if s[ 5 ][ 8 ] == s[4][2]:
    print ( ' Same Gender ' )
else:
    print ( " False " )
```

Output:

```
Same Gender
```

Chapter 12

Statistics

Statistics is the practice of gathering and analyzing large quantities of data to get information. Statistics are used to answer important questions on data, especially population questions. It provides a structured approach to solving each question, not based on bias and intuition. However, statistics as a topic is very wide and has numerous libraries so there is no direct or single way to approach problems statistically. It's easy to input the data but not so easy to calculate and justify the results of the calculation with the various methods available. This chapter is going to focus on two major types of descriptive statistics. It will discuss their relevance and the way to achieve them in Python. It will also focus on some of the most powerful statistical libraries and tools in the Python arsenal. It will discuss how to the libraries work and the ways to use them productively.

Descriptive Statistics

Descriptive statistics is used to characterize and summarize a given set of data based on its properties. Basically, it describes the main features of the given data by producing short summaries of the data. There are four different ways in which descriptive statistics can be classified:

1.   Measures of Central Tendency

2. Measures of Position

3. Measures of Variation or Spread

4. Measures of Frequency

This chapter will focus on the measures of central tendency and variation.

Measures of Central Tendency

There are three measures of central tendency – the mean, median, and mode. In a given set of data with n number of values and x_i *as the* total sum of values, the mean, μ, is the total sum of values x_i divided by the number of values n i.e.

$$\mu = \frac{xi}{n}$$

The words "mean" and "average" are sometimes used interchangeably, but they might not necessarily mean the same thing. The best word to describe an output obtained with the formula above is mean.

To calculate the mean of a given data in Python, a function which specifies the parameter that correlates with the formula above must be defined. For example,

```
def mean( y ) :
x = sum( y ) / len( y )
        print ( x )
        return
```

Example

1. Analyze the data gathered from a group of workers during health week.

S/N	1	2	3	4	5	6	7	8	9	10
Age	32	26	45	54	27	21	28	23	26	30
Weight (kg)	81	61	74	72	75	65	80	68	78	83
Height (cm)	164	165	171	170	179	177	187	`155	180	185

Calculate the mean age, weight, and height.

```
Solution:
from _future_ import division
# remember that the division operator won't work
in Python 2.7 without the import
def mean( y ) :
x = sum( y ) / len( y )
        print ( x )
        return
Age = [ 32, 26, 45, 54, 27, 21, 28, 23, 26, 30]
Weight = [ 81, 61, 74, 72, 75, 65, 80, 68, 78,
83 ]
Height = [ 164, 165, 171, 170, 179, 177, 187,
155, 180, 185 ]
mean( Age )
mean( Height )
mean( Weight )
```

Output:

```
31.2
173.3
73.7
```

The next measure is the median. The median refers to the middle value in a given set of data. Selecting the median of a data is quite tricky because it works based on the order the values are assigned to the variable. It's best to calculate the median of an ordered set of data rather than random. The function to calculate the median is defined as:

```
def median( y ):
y = len( y )
sorted_y = sorted( y )
midpoint = y // 2
if    n % 2 == 1:
# this instructs the interpreter to return the
middle value if odd
return sorted_y [ midpoint ]
else:
        less = midpoint - 1
        high = midpoint
        print (sorted_y [ less ] + sorted_y [ high
]) / 2
        return
```

Example:

Calculate the median age of the data gathered from the workers during the health week.

Solution:

```python
from _future_ import division
def median( y ):
    g = len( y )
    sorted_y = sorted(y)
# this arranges the data from smallest to largest
    midpoint = g // 2
    if      g % 2 == 1:
# this instructs the interpreter to return the middle value if odd
        print ( sorted_y [ midpoint ] )
        return
    else:
        less = midpoint - 1
        high = midpoint
        i = sorted_y [ less ] + sorted_y [ high ]
        j = i / 2
        print ( j )
Age = [ 32, 26, 45, 54, 27, 21, 28, 23, 26, 30]
Weight = [ 81, 61, 74, 72, 75, 65, 80, 68, 78, 83 ]
Height = [ 164, 165, 171, 170, 179, 177, 187, 155, 180, 185 ]
median ( Age )
median ( Weight )
median ( Height )
```

Output:

```
27.5
74.5
174.0
```

Measures of Variation or Spread

Variance

While mean describes the central tendency of a set of values, variance describes the spread. The variance of a given set of values is calculated as

$$\sigma^2 = \frac{1}{n}\Sigma_i(xi - \mu)^2$$

The term 'xi-μ' represents the "mean deviation," so the variance of a data set is the mean of squared mean deviation of the data and it is denoted as σ^2. The square root of variance, σ, is called the standard deviation.

The general syntax of a function that calculates standard deviation and variance:

```
def mean_deviation( p ):
   p_bar = mean(p)
   return  [p_i  -  p_bar for  p_i   in    p]
def variance(p):
   n = len(p)
   deviations  =     mean_deviation(p)
   o = sum_of_squares(deviations) / (n - 1)
   print (" The variance is " + 0)
   standard_deviation = sqrt( o ) #the function for
   squareroot
```

```python
print (" The standard deviation is   "
+standard_deviation )
```

Write a program that calculates the mean, median, variance and standard deviation of the data gathered from a group of workers during health week.

Solution:

```python
from _future_ import division
def mean( y ) :
   x = sum( y ) / len( y )
        print ( x )
        return
def mean_deviation( p ):
        p_bar = mean(p)
        return [p_i - p _bar    for  p_i  in  p]
    def    variance(p):
        n = len(p)
        deviations  =       mean_deviation(p)
        o = sum_of_squares(deviations) / (n - 1)
        print (" The variance is " + 0)
        standard_deviation = sqrt( o ) #the
        function for squareroot
        print (" The standard deviation is   "
        +standard_deviation )
    def median( y ):
        g = len( y )
        sorted_y = sorted(y)
# this arranges the data from smallest to
largest
        midpoint = g // 2
        if      g % 2 == 1:
# this instructs the interpreter to return the
middle value if odd
```

```python
            print ( sorted_y [ midpoint ] )
            return
        else:
            less = midpoint - 1
            high = midpoint
        i = sorted_y [ less ] + sorted_y [ high ]
        j = i / 2
            print ( j )
Age = [ 32, 26, 45, 54, 27, 21, 28, 23, 26, 30]
Weight = [ 81, 61, 74, 72, 75, 65, 80, 68, 78,
83 ]
Height = [ 164, 165, 171, 170, 179, 177, 187,
155, 180, 185 ]
mean ( Age )
mean ( Weight )
mean ( Height )
median ( Age )
median ( Weight )
median ( Height )
variance ( Age )
variance ( Weight )
variance ( Height )
```

Output:

```
31.2
173.3
73.7

27.5
74.5
174.0

The variance is 44.222222222222214
The variance is 66.2222222222223
The variance is 97.33333333333333
```

```
The standard deviation is 6.6499791144420001
The standard deviation is 8.137703743822469
The standard deviation is 9.865765724632494
```

Statistical Libraries in Python

1. SciPy

While Numpy contains some standard statistical functions, the real reservoir of statistical functions is contained in the scipy module. The install statement of the module can be found on the website. Scipy.stats has over eighty different continuous probability distribution, ten discrete probability distributions, and numerous supplementary functions to select from. To access the module, it's easier to create an object that represents the distribution you plan to use. For example,

```
>>> import scipy.stats  # this method is a bit
slower, it's easier to
>>> d = scipy.stats.norm( 0, 8 )
```

The variable d is created as a normally distributed variable with standard deviation $\sigma = 8$, and mean $= 0$. The parameters are sometimes referred to as scale (standard deviation) and location (mean). Once defined the mean can be computed as the following:

```
>>> d.mean( ) # from it's definition, it's equal
to 0
```

Higher order moments can be computed as :

```
>>> d.moment(4)
30000
```

The main functions used to define random variables are :

- ❖ stats: variance, (Fisher's) skewness, or kurtosis, and mean

- ❖ cdf: cumulative distribution function

- ❖ sf: survival function (1-cdf)

- ❖ ppf: percent point function (Inverse of cdf)

- ❖ isf: inverse survival function (Inverse of sf)

- ❖ pdf: probability density function

- ❖ rvs: random variates

- ❖ moment: non-central moments of the distribution

Example

```
>>> d.cdf(0)
    0.5                 # or the pdf of the same object
>>> d.pdf(0)
    0.039894228040143268
```

Samples can be created from the distribution:

```
>>> d.rvs(10)
```

Most popular statistical tests are customarily integrated into the module. An example is the Shapiro-Wilks test which tests for null hypothesis on data extracted from a normal distribution, for example

```
>>> scipy.stats.shapiro( n.rvs( 100 ) )
    ( 0.9914381704058838, 0.779195349080658 )
```

The second output in the tuple is called the p-value.

2. SymPy

The SymPy module is a much smaller library, containing lesser but extremely powerful functions that allows the manipulation of statistical values. Example,

```
>>> from sympy import stats
>>> b = stats.Normal( 'x', 1, 9) # to create a
normal random variable
```

The probability density function can be acquired by

```
>>> from sympy.abc import x
>>> stats.density( X ) ( x ) sqrt(2) * exp( -
x**2 / 200 ) / ( 20 * sqrt ( pi ) )        # sqrt
performs the squareroot operation in Python
```

and the cumulative density function can be evaluated as the follows,

```
>>> stats.cdf ( X ) ( 0 ) 1 /2
```

This can be evaluated numerically with the evalf( ) function on the output of the code. SymPy is designed to solve probability 'P' questions intuitively by using the stats.P method. For example,

```
>>> stats.P( X > 0 )
    1/2
```

The corresponding expectation stats.E   function is used to solve complex expectations by utilizing every machinery available in SymPy's arsenal. To evaluate $E\left(\sqrt{|X|}\right)$ in Python,

```
>>> stats.E( abs ( X ) ** ( 1 / 2 ) ) .evalf( )
    2.59995915343879
```

Other Modules Used in Python for Statistics

There are various modules that can be used to solve statistical problems in Python. Seaborn and Statsmodels are excellent examples of such modules. Seaborn is a library similar to Matplotlib with it's detailed and demonstrative statistical visualizations. It is used majorly for data exploration activities. Statsmodels was created to provide additional support for SciPy's library with functions that carry out estimation, interference, and descriptive statistics for various statistical data. With Statsmodel, there is an emphasis on solving econometric problems with generalized and robust linear models.

Statsmodel and Seaborn are both well-accepted among data scientists and they were constructed to blend well with the existing Python libraries such as Numpy, Scipy, and Matplotlib and various others.

Chapter 13

Probability

In grade school, you were introduced to the natural numbers (i.e., 1,2,3,...) and you learned how to manipulate them by operations like addition, subtraction, and multiplication. Later, you were introduced to positive and negative numbers and were again taught how to manipulate them. Ultimately, you were introduced to the calculus of the real line and learned how to differentiate, take limits, and so on.

This progression provided more abstractions but also widened the field of problems you could successfully tackle. The same is true of probability. One way to think about probability is as a new number concept that allows you to tackle problems that have a special kind of uncertainty built into them.

Thus, the key idea is that there is some number, say x, with a traveling companion, say, f (x), and this companion represents the uncertainties about the value of x as if looking at the number x through a frosted window. The degree of opacity of the window is represented by f (x). To manipulate x, then you have to figure out what to do with f (x). For example, if you want y = 2x, then you have to understand how f (x) generates f (y). Another good example is a beehive with the swarm around it representing f (x), and the hive itself, which you can barely see through the swarm, as x. The random part is that you don't know which bee, in particular, is going to sting you! Once this happens the uncertainty evaporates. Up until that happens, all you have is a concept of a swarm (i.e., the density of bees) which represents a potentiality of which bee will ultimately sting.

In summary, one way to think about probability is as a way of carrying through mathematical reasoning (e.g., adding, subtracting, taking limits) with a notion of potentiality that is so-transformed by these operations.

Understanding Probability Density

In order to understand the heart of modern probability, which is built on the Lebesgue theory of integration. First, there is a need to extend the concept of integration from rudimentary calculus. Starting with the following piecewise function,

$$f(y) = \begin{cases} 1 & \\ 2 & \text{if } 0 < y \leq 1 \\ 0 & \text{if } 1 < y \leq 2 \end{cases}$$

In calculus, you learned Riemann integration, which you can apply here as

$$\int_0^2 f(x)dx = 1 + 2 = 3$$

which has the usual interpretation as the area of the two rectangles that make up $f(x)$. So far, so good.

With Lebesgue integration, the idea is very similar except that you focus on the y-axis rather than moving along the x-axis. The question is given $f(x) = 1$, what is the set of x values for which this is true? For example, this is true whenever $x \in (0,1]$. So now there's a correspondence between the values of the function (namely, 1 and 2) and the sets of x values for which this is true, namely, $\{(0,1]\}$ and $\{(1,2]\}$, respectively.

To compute the integral, you simply take the function values (i.e., 1, 2) and some way of measuring the size of the corresponding interval (i.e., μ) as in the following:

$$\int_0^2 f d\mu \;=\; 1\mu(\{(0,1]\}) + 2\mu(\{(1,2]\})$$

Some of the notations above have been suppressed to emphasize generality.

NB: The same value of the integral as in the Riemann case when $\mu((0,1]) = \mu((1,2]) = 1$ was obtained.

By introducing the μ function as a way of measuring the intervals above, you have introduced another degree of freedom in the integration. This accommodates many weird functions that are not tractable using the usual Riemann theory. Nonetheless, the key step in the above discussion is the introduction of the μ function, which you will encounter again as the so-called probability density function.

Random Variables

Most introductions to probability jump straight into random variables and then explain how to compute complicated integrals. The problem with this approach is that it skips over some of the important subtleties that will be considered now. Unfortunately, the term random variable is not very descriptive. The better term is a measurable function. To understand why this is a better term, it's necessary to dive into the formal constructions of probability by way of a simple example. Consider tossing a fair six-sided die. There are only six outcomes possible,

$$\Omega = \{\, 1, 2, 3, 4, 5, 6\}$$

As you know, if the die is fair, then the probability of each outcome is 1/6. To say this formally, the measure of each set (i.e., $\{1\},\{2\},...,$ to $\{6\}$) is $\mu(\{1\}) = \mu(\{2\})...= $ to $\mu(\{6\})$ is equal to 1/6. In this case, the μ function discussed earlier is the usual probability mass function, denoted by P. The measurable function maps a set into a number on the real line. For example, $\{1\} \rightarrow 1$ is one such uninteresting function.

Things are about to get more interesting. Suppose you were asked to construct a fair coin from the fair die. In other words, you're to throw the die and then record the outcomes as if you had just tossed a fair coin. How will you do this?

One way would be to define a measurable function that says if the die comes up 3 or less, then you declare heads and otherwise declare tails. This strategy creates two different non-overlapping sets $\{1,2,3\}$ and $\{4,5,6\}$. Each set has the same probability measure,

$$P(\{1,2,3\}) = 1/2$$

$$P(\{4,5,6\}) = 1/2$$

And the problem is solved. Every time the die comes up $\{1,2,3\}$ record heads, and record tails otherwise.

Is this the only way to construct a fair coin experiment from a fair die?

Alternatively, you can define the sets as $\{1\}$, $\{2\}$, $\{3,4,5,6\}$. The corresponding measure for each set can be defined as the following

$$P(\{1\}) = 1/2$$

$$P(\{2\}) = 1/2$$

$$P(\{3,4,5,6\}) = 0$$

then, leading to another solution to the fair coin problem. To implement this, all you need to do is ignore every time the die shows 3,4,5,6 and throw again. This is wasteful, but it solves the problem.

There's a slightly more interesting problem when you toss two dice. Assume that each throw is independent, meaning that the outcome of one does not influence the other.

What are the sets in this case? They are all pairs of possible outcomes from two throws as shown below,

$$\Omega = \{(1,1),(1,2),...,(5,6),(6,6)\}$$

What are the measures of each of these sets? By virtue of the independence claim, the measure of each is the product of the respective measures of each element. For instance,

$$P((1,2)) = P(\{1\})\,P(\{2\}) = \frac{1}{6^2}$$

With all that's established, it's easy to answer the following question: what is the probability that the sum of the dice equals seven? The first thing to do is characterize the measurable function for this as

$$X : (a,b) \rightarrow (a+b).$$

Next, you associate all of the (a, b) pairs with their sum. A Python dictionary can be created for this as shown below,

```
d={(a,b):a+b
        for i in range(1,7)
            for j in range(1,7)}
```

The next step is to collect all of the (a,b) pairs that sum to each of the possible values from two to twelve.

```
from collections import defaultdict
dinv = defaultdict(list)
for i,j in d.iteritems():
        dinv[ j ].append( I )
```

Convergence

The exclusion of probability density in raw data is a sign that the sequence of random variables should be argued in an organized order. An expression in rudimentary calculus,

$$xn \rightarrow xo$$

which represents 'xn', the real number sequence. This means that for any given $\in > 0$, no matter how small, you can exhibit a m such that for any n > m, you have

$$|xn - xo| < \in$$

Intuitively, this means that once you get past m in the sequence, you get as to within Σ of xo. This means that nothing surprising happens in the sequence on the long march to infinity, which gives a sense of uniformity to the convergence process. When arguing about convergence for statistics, you want the same look-and-feel as you have here, but because this is about random variables, there is nea ed for other concepts. There are two moving parts for random variables. Recall that random variables are really functions that map sets into the real line:

$$X : \Omega \rightarrow R .$$

Thus, one part to keep track of is the behavior of the subsets of Ω while arguing about convergence. The other part is the sequence of values that the random variable takes on the real line and how those behave in the convergence process.

Almost Sure Convergence

The most straightforward extension into statistics of this convergence concept is convergence with probability one, which is also known as almost sure convergence, which is the following,

$$P\{\text{for each } \in > 0 \text{ there is } n \in > 0 \text{ such that for all } n > n \in, |Xn - X| < \in \} = 1$$

Note the similarity to the prior notion of convergence for real numbers. When this happens, you write this as $X_n \rightarrow X$. In this context, almost sure convergence means that if you take any particular $\omega \in \Omega$ and then look at the sequence of real numbers that are produced by each of the random variables,

$$(X1(\omega), X2(\omega), X3(\omega),...,Xn(\omega))$$

then this sequence is just a real-valued sequence in the sense of the convergence on the real line and convergence in the same way. If you collect all of the ω for which this is true and the measure of that collection equals one, then you have almost sure convergence of the random variable. Notice how the convergence idea applies to both sides of the random variable: the (domain) Ω side and the (codomain) real-valued side. An equivalent and more compact way of writing this is the following,

$$P\left(\omega \in \Omega: \lim_{n\to\infty} X_n(\omega) = X(\omega) \right) = 1$$

Example

To get the feel for the mechanics of this kind of convergence, consider the following sequence of uniformly distributed random variables on the unit interval, $X_n \sim U[0,1]$. Now, consider taking the maximum of the set of n such variables as the following,

$$X_{(n)} = \max\{X_1, ..., X_n\}$$

In other words, you scan through a list of n uniformly distributed random variables and pick out the maximum over the set. Intuitively, you should expect that $X_{(n)}$ should somehow converge to one. You can also make this happen almost surely, exhibit m so that the following is true,

$$P(|1- X(n)|) < \epsilon \text{ when } n > m$$

Because $X_{(n)} < 1$, you can simplify this as the following,

$$1- P(X_{(n)} < \epsilon) = 1-(1-\epsilon)^m \xrightarrow[m\to\infty]{} 1$$

Thus, this sequence converges almost surely. You can work this example out in Python using Scipy to make it concrete with the following code,

```
>>> from scipy import stats
>>> u=stats.uniform( )
 >>> xn = lambda i: u.rvs(i).max()
>>> xn(5) 0.96671783848200299
```

Thus, the x_n variable is the same as the $X_{(n)}$ random variable in the example.

There are still some cases where a particular realization will skip below the line. To get the probability guarantee of the definition satisfied, you have to make sure that for whatever n_ϵ you settle on, the probability of this kind of noncompliant behavior should be extremely small, say, less than 1%. Now, you can compute the following to estimate this probability for $n = 60$ over 1000 realizations,

```
>>> import numpy as np
>>> np.mean([xn(60) > 0.95 for i in range(1000)])
0.96099999999999997
```

So, the probability of having a noncompliant case beyond $n > 60$ is pretty good, but not still the major plan (0.99). You can solve for the m in the analytic proof of convergence by plugging in the factors for ϵ and the desired probability constraint,

```
>>> print np.log(1-.99)/np.log(.95)
89.7811349607
```

Now, rounding this up and re-visiting the same estimate as above,

```
>>> import numpy as np
>>> np.mean([xn(90) > 0.95 for i in range(1000)])
0.995
```

which is the ultimate result. The important thing to understand from this example is that there is need to select convergence criteria for both the values of the random variable (0.95) and for the probability of achieving that level (0.99) in order to compute the m. Informally speaking, almost sure convergence means that not only will any particular X_n be close to X for large n, but the whole sequence of values will remain close to X with high probability.

Convergence in Probability

A weaker kind of convergence is convergence in probability, which means the following:

$$P\left(\mid X_n - X \mid > \epsilon\right) \rightarrow 0$$

as $n \rightarrow \infty$ for each $\epsilon > 0$.

This is notationally shown as $X_n \rightarrow X$. For example, consider the following sequence of random variables where $X_n = 1/2^n$ with probability pn and where $X_n = c$ with probability $1 - pn$. Then X_n P $\rightarrow 0$ as $p_n \rightarrow 1$. This is allowable under this notion of convergence because a diminishing amount of non- converging behavior (namely, when $X_n = c$) is possible.

Example

To get some sense of the mechanics of this kind of convergence, let {X1, X2, X3,...} be the indicators of the corresponding intervals,

$$(0,1],(0,\ 1\ 2],(1\ 2,1],(0,\ 1\ 3],(1\ 3,\ 2\ 3],(2\ 3,1]$$

Solution:

Keep splitting the unit interval into equal chunks and enumerate those chunks with X_i. Because each X_i is an indicator function, it takes only two values: zero and one. For example, for $X2 = 1$ if $0 < x \leq 1/2$ and zero otherwise.

NB: x ~U(0,1). Which means that $P(X2 = 1) = 1/2$.

To compute the sequence of $P(Xn > \epsilon)$ for each n for some $\epsilon \in$ (0,1). For X_1, $P(X1 > \epsilon) = 1$ because ϵ in the interval is covered by X_1. For X_2, $P(X2 > \epsilon) = 1/2$, for X3, $P(X3 > \epsilon) = 1/3$, and so on. This produces the following sequence: (1, 1 2, 1 2, 1 3, 1 3,...). The limit of the sequence is zero so that X_n P → 0. However, for every x $\in$ (0,1), the sequence of function values of $X_n(x)$ consists of infinitely many zeros and ones (remember that indicator functions can evaluate to either zero or one). Thus, the set of x for which the sequence $X_n(x)$ converges is empty because the sequence bounces between zero and one. This means that almost sure convergence fails here even though there is convergence in probability. The key distinction is that convergence in probability considers the convergence of a sequence of probabilities whereas almost sure convergence is concerned about the sequence of values of the random variables over sets of events that fill out the underlying probability space entirely (i.e., with probability one). This is a very good example that can be integrated into Python. The following is a function to compute the different subintervals,

```
>>>         make_interval=      lambda       n:
np.array(zip(range(n+1),range(1,n+1)))/n
>>> intervals= np.vstack([make_interval(i) for i
in range(1,5)])
>>> print intervals
[[ 0.            1.            ]
 [ 0.            0.5           ]
 [ 0.5          1.            ]
 [ 0.            0.33333333    ]
 [ 0.33333333   0.66666667    ]
 [ 0.66666667   1.            ]
```

```
[ 0.        0.25      ]
[ 0.25      0.5       ]
[ 0.5       0.75      ]
[ 0.75      1.        ]]
```

The following function computes the bit string in the example, {X1, X2,...,Xn},

```
>>> bits= lambda u:((intervals[:,0] < u) &
(u<=intervals[:,1])).astype(int)
>>> bits(u.rvs()) array([1, 0, 1, 0, 0, 1, 0, 0,
0, 1])
```

Now that the individual bit strings is available, the next objective is to show convergence and that the probability of each entry goes to a limit. For example, using ten realizations,

```
>>> print np.vstack([bits(u.rvs()) for i in
range(10)])
[ [1 1 0 1 0 0 0 1 0 0]
[1 1 0 1 0 0 0 1 0 0]
[1 1 0 0 1 0 0 1 0 0]
[1 0 1 0 0 1 0 0 1 0]
[1 0 1 0 0 1 0 0 1 0]
[1 1 0 0 1 0 0 1 0 0]
[1 1 0 1 0 0 1 0 0 0]
[1 1 0 0 1 0 0 1 0 0]
[1 1 0 0 1 0 0 1 0 0]
[1 1 0 1 0 0 1 0 0 0] ]
```

The goal is for the limiting probability of a 1 in each column to convert to a limit. This can estimate over 1000 realizations using the following code,

```
>>> np.vstack([bits(u.rvs()) for i in
range(1000)]).mean(axis=0) array([ 1. , 0.493,
```

0.507, 0.325, 0.34 , 0.335, 0.253, 0.24 , 0.248,
0.259])

NB:

- These entries should approach the (1, 1 2, 1 2, 1 3, 1 3,...)sequence found earlier.
- The individual sequences of zeros and ones do not converge, but the probabilities of these sequences converge. This is the key difference between almost sure convergence and convergence in probability.

Thus, convergence in probability does not imply almost sure convergence. Conversely, almost sure convergence does imply convergence in probability.

Chapter 14

Machine Learning

Machine Learning is a wide and growing subject. It's impossible to cover even a quarter of it in this chapter. However, this chapter will cover the important topics you need to know to get started with machine learning. Machine learning and statistics have the same problem- how to make data actionable. Statistics solves it by creating powerful analytic estimators while machine learning answers with predictive analytics.

Python provides many bindings for machine learning libraries, some specialized for technologies such as neural networks, and others geared towards novice users. This chapter will focus on the powerful and popular Scikit-learn module. Scikit-learn is distinguished by its consistent and sensible API, its wealth of machine learning algorithms, its clear documentation, and its readily available datasets that make it easy to follow along with the online documentation. Like Pandas, Scikit-learn relies on Numpy for numerical arrays. Since its release in 2007, Scikit-learn has become the most widely used, general purpose, open source machine learning modules that is popular in both industry and academia. Scikit-learn can be downloaded at the website.

How to use Scikit

First thing to do is to create data for linear regression:

```
>>> import numpy as np
>>> from matplotlib.pylab import subplots
>>>      from      sklearn.linear_model      import
LinearRegression
>>> X = np.arange(10) # create some data
>>> Y = X+np.random.randn (10)  # linear with
noise
```

Next import and create an instance of the Linear Regression class from Scikit-learn.

```
>>> from sklearn.linear_model import
LinearRegression
>>> lr=LinearRegression() # create model
```

Scikit-learn has a wonderfully consistent API. All Scikit-learn objects use the fit method to compute model parameters and the predict method to evaluate the model. For the Linear Regression instance,the fit method computes the coefficients of the linear fit. This method requires a matrix of inputs where the rows are the samples and the columns are the features. The target of the regression are the Y values, which must be correspondingly shaped, as in the following,

```
>>> X,Y = X.reshape((-1,1)), Y.reshape((-1,1))
>>> lr.fit(X,Y)
LinearRegression(copy_X=True,
fit_intercept=True, normalize=False)
>>> lr.coef_
array([[ 0.94211853]])
```

The `coef_property` of the linear regression object shows the estimated parameters for the fit. The convention is to denote estimated parameters with a trailing underscore. The model has a score method that computes the R2 value for the regression.

```
>>> lr.score(X,Y) 0.9059042979442371
```

Now, that it's fitted, the fit can be evaluated using the predict method,

```
>>> xi = np.linspace(0,10,15) # more points to draw
>>> xi = xi.reshape((-1,1)) # reshape as columns
>>> yp = lr.predict(xi)
```

Multilinear Regression

The Scikit-learn module easily extends linear regression to multiple dimensions. For example, for multi-linear regression,

$$y = \alpha_0 + \alpha_1 x_1 + \alpha_2 x_2 + \cdots + \alpha_n x_n$$

The problem is to find all of the α terms given the training set $\{x_1, x_2,...,x_n, y\}$. To create another sample data set:

```
>>> X = np.random.randint(20,size=(10,2))
>>> Y = X.dot([1, 3])+1 +
np.random.randn(X.shape[0])*20
>>> lr=LinearRegression()
>>> lr.fit(X,Y) LinearRegression(copy_X=True,
fit_intercept=True, normalize=False)
>>> print lr.coef_ [ 0.35171694 4.04064287]
```

The `coef_` variable now has two terms in it, corresponding to the two input dimensions. The constant offset is already built-in and is an option on the Linear Regression constructor.

Polynomial Regression

The data above can extend to include polynomial regression by using the polynomial features in the preprocessing sub-module. To keep it simple, let's go back to the one-dimensional example. First, create synthetic data,

```
from sklearn.preprocessing import
PolynomialFeatures
X = np.arange(10).reshape(-1,1) # create some
data
Y = X+X**2+X**3+ np.random.randn(*X.shape)*80
# next create a transformation from X to a
polynomial of X
qfit = PolynomialFeatures(degree=2) # quadratic
Xq = qfit.fit_transform(X)
print Xq
```

Output:

```
[ [ 1.   0.   0.]
  [ 1.   1.   1.]
  [ 1.   2.   4.]
  [ 1.   3.   9.]
  [ 1.   4. 16.]
  [ 1.   5. 25.]
  [ 1.   6. 36.]
  [ 1.   7. 49.]
  [ 1.   8. 64.]
  [ 1.   9. 81.] ]
```

Note that there is an automatic constant term in the output 0th column where fit_ transform has mapped the single-column input into a set of columns representing the individual polynomial terms. The middle column has the linear term, and the last has the quadratic term. With these polynomial features stacked as columns of Xq, all you have to do is fit and predict again. The following draws a comparison between the linear regression and the quadratic repression.

```
>>> lr=LinearRegression() # create linear model
>>> qr=LinearRegression() # create quadratic
model
>>> lr.fit(X,Y) # fit linear model
LinearRegression(copy_X=True,
fit_intercept=True, normalize=False)
>>> qr.fit(Xq,Y) # fit quadratic model
LinearRegression(copy_X=True,
fit_intercept=True, normalize=False)
>>> lp = lr.predict(xi) >>> qp =
qr.predict(qfit.fit_transform(xi))
```

This just scratches the surface of Scikit-learn. A lot of examples are available on the internet if you need more practice but the main thing is to concentrate on the usage (i.e., fit, predict) which is standardized across all of the machine learning methods that are implemented in Scikit-learn.

Theory of Learning

There is nothing so practical as a good theory. In this section, the formal framework for thinking about machine learning will be established. This framework will help you think beyond particular methods for machine learning so you can integrate new methods or combine existing methods intelligently. Both machine learning and statistics share the common goal of trying to derive understanding from data. Some historical perspective helps. Most of the methods in statistics were derived towards the start of the 20th century when data were hard to come by.

Society was preoccupied with the potential dangers of human overpopulation and work was focused on studying agriculture and crop yields. At this time, even a dozen data points was considered plenty. Around the same time, the deep foundations of probability were being established by Kolmogorov. Thus, the lack of data meant that the conclusions had to be buttressed by strong assumptions and solid mathematics provided by the emerging theory of probability. Furthermore, inexpensive powerful computers were not yet widely available.

The situation today is much different: there are lots of data collected and powerful and easily programmable computers are available. The important problems no longer revolve around a dozen data points on a farm acre, but rather millions of points on a square millimeter of a DNA microarray. Does this mean that statistics will be superseded by machine learning? In contrast to classical statistics, which is concerned with developing models that characterize, explain, and describe phenomena, machine learning is primarily concerned with prediction, usually at the expense of all else.

Areas like exploratory statistics are very closely related to machine learning, but the degree of emphasis on prediction is still distinguishing. In some sense, this is unavoidable due to the size of the data machine learning can reduce. In other words, machine learning can help distill a table of a million columns into one hundred columns, but is it still possible to interpret one hundred columns meaningfully? In classical statistics, this was never an issue because data were of a much smaller scale. Whereas mathematical models, usually normal distributions, fitted with observations are common in statistics, machine learning uses data to construct models that sit on complicated data structures and exploit nonlinear optimizations that lack closed-form solutions.

A common maxim is that statistics is data plus analytical theory and machine learning is data plus computable structures. This makes it seem like machine learning is completely ad-hoc and devoid of the underlying theory, but this is not the case, and both machine learning and statistics share many important theoretical results.

Introduction to Theory of Machine Learning

The syntax of storing a machine learning problem. Define the unknown target function, $f : X \rightarrow Y$. The training set is $\{(x, y)\}$ which means that only the function's inputs/outputs can be seen. The hypothesis set H is the set of all possible guesses at f. This is the set that the final estimate f will been drawn the final estimate. The machine learning problem is how to derive the best element from the hypothesis set by using the training set.

Example

Suppose X consists of all three-bit vectors (i.e., X = $\{000,001,....,111\}$) as in the code below,

```
import pandas as pd
import numpy as np
from pandas import DataFrame
df=DataFrame(index=pd.Index(['{0:04b}'.format(i)
for i in range(2**4)],
        dtype='str',
        name='x'),columns=['f'])
```

Next, define the target function f below which just checks if the number of zeros in the binary representation exceeds the number of

ones. If so, then the function outputs 1 and 0 otherwise (i.e.,Y
$=\{0,1\}$).

```
df.f=np.array(df.index.map(lambda
i:i.count('0'))
        df.index.map(lambda
i:i.count('1')),dtype=int)
df.head(8) # show top half only
f

x
0000   1
0001   1
0010   1
0011   0
0100   1
0101   0
0110   0
0111   0
```

The hypothesis set for this problem is the set of all possible functions of X. The set D represents all possible input/output pairs. The corresponding hypothesis set H has 216 elements, one of which matches f . There are 216 elements in the hypothesis set because for each of sixteen input elements, there are two possible corresponding values zero or one for each input. Thus, the size of the hypothesis set is $2\times2\times\cdots\times 2 = 216$. Now, presented with a training set consisting of the first eight input/output pairs, the goal is to minimize errors over the training set ($E_{in}(\,f\,)$). There are 28 elements from the hypothesis set that exactly match f over the training set. There is a need for another element in the problem in order to proceed. The extra piece is needed to assume that the training set represents a random sampling (in-sample data) from a greater population (out-of-sample data) that would be consistent with the population that f would ultimately predict upon.

There is a subtle consequence of this assumption—whatever the machine learning method does once deployed, in order for it to continue to work, it cannot disturb the data environment that it was trained on. Said differently, if the method is not to be trained continuously, then it cannot break this assumption by altering the generative environment that produced the data it was trained on. For example, suppose a model that predicts hospital readmissions based on seasonal weather and patient health is developed. Because the model is so effective, in the next six months, the hospital forestalls readmissions by delivering interventions that improve patient health. Clearly using the model cannot change seasonal weather, but because the hospital used the model to change patient health, the training data used to build the model is no longer consistent with the forward-looking health of the patients. Thus, there is little reason to think that the model will continue to work as well going forward.

Returning to the previous example, suppose that the first eight elements from X are twice as likely as the last eight. The following code is a function that generates elements from X according to this distribution.

```python
np.random.seed(12)
def get_sample(n=1): ...
    if n==1:
        return'{0:04b}'.format(np.random.choice(range(
        8)*2+range(8,16)))
    else:
        return [get_sample(1) for _ in range(n)]
```

The next block applies the function definition f to the sampled data to generate the training set consisting of eight elements.

```python
train=df.f.ix[get_sample(8)]       #        8-element
training set
train.index.unique().shape  # how  many  unique
elements?  (6,)
```

Notice that even though there are eight elements, there is redundancy because these are drawn according to an underlying probability. Otherwise, there are just sixteen different elements and a training set consisting of the complete specification of f and then it would be clear which h $\in$H to pick! However, this effect gives a clue as to how it will ultimately work.

Given the elements in the training set, consider the set of elements from the hypothesis set that exactly match. How to choose among these? The answer is it does not matter! Why? Because under the assumption that the prediction will be used in an environment that is determined by the same probability, getting something outside of the training set is just as likely as getting something inside the training set. The size of the training set is key here— the bigger the training set, the less likely that there will be real-world data that fall outside of it and the better f will perform. The following code shows the elements of the training set in the context of all possible data.

This assumes that the hypothesis set is big enough to capture the entire training set (which it is for this example).

```python
df['fhat']=df.f.ix[train.index.unique()]
df.fhat
x
0000 NaN
```

```
0001 NaN
0010 1
0011 0
0100 1
0101 NaN
0110 0
0111 NaN
1000 1
1001 0
1010 NaN
1011 NaN
1100 NaN
1101 NaN
1110 NaN
1111 NaN
Name: fhat, dtype: float64
```

NB: There are NaN symbols where the training set had no values. For definiteness, you can fill these in with zeros, although you can fill them with anything you want so long as whatever you do is not determined by the training set.

```
df.fhat.fillna(0,inplace=True) #final
specification of fhat
```

Now, pretend you have deployed this and generate some test data.

```
test= df.f.ix[get_sample(50)]
  (df.ix[test.index]['fhat'] != test).mean()
0.17999999999999999
```

The result shows the error rate, given the probability mechanism that is generating the data. The following Pandas-fu compares the overlap between the training set and the test set in the context of all possible data. The NaN values show the rows where the test data

had items absent in the training data. Recall that the method returns
zero for these items. As shown, sometimes this works in its favor,
and sometimes not.

```
pd.concat([test.groupby(level=0).mean(),
           train.groupby(level=0).mean()],
          axis=1,
          keys=['test','train'])
          test train
0000 1 NaN
0001 1 NaN
0010 1 1
0011 0 0
0100 1 1
0101 0 NaN
0110 0 0
0111 0 NaN
1000 1 1
1001 0 0
1010 0 NaN
1011 0 NaN
1100 0 NaN
1101 0 NaN
1110 0 NaN
1111 0 NaN
```

Note that where the test data and training data share elements, they
agree. When the test set produced an unseen element, it produces a
match or not. Now, you are in the position to ask how big the
training set should be to achieve a level of performance.

For example, on average, how many in-samples are needed for a
given error rate? For this problem, you can ask how large (on
average) must the training set be in order to capture all of the

possibilities and achieve perfect out- of-sample error rates? For this problem, this turns out to be sixty-three.

```
>>> train=df.f.ix[get_sample(63)]
>>> del df['fhat']
>>> df['fhat']=df.f.ix[train.index.unique()]
>>> df.fhat.fillna(0,inplace=True) #final
specification of fhat
>>> test= df.f.ix[get_sample(50)]
>>> (df.fhat.ix[test] != df.f.ix[test]).mean() #
error rate 0.0
```

Notice that this bigger training set has a better error rate because it is able to identify the best element from the hypothesis set because the training set captured more of the complexity of the unknown f. This example shows the trade-offs between the size of the training set, the complexity of the target function, the probability structure of the data, and the size of the hypothesis set.

Theory of Generalization

The main question is how the method will perform once deployed. It would be nice to have some kind of performance guarantee. In other words, after working hard to minimize the errors in the training set, what errors can you expect at deployment? In training, the in-sample error, $E_{in}(f)$ is minimized, but that's not good enough. There should be guarantees about the out-of-sample error, $E_{out}(f)$. This is what generalization means in machine learning. The mathematical statement of this is the following,

$$P\left(E_{out}(\hat{f}) - E_{in}(\hat{f})| > \epsilon\right) < \delta$$

for a given ϵ and δ. Informally, this says that the probability of the respective errors differing by more than a given ϵ is less than some quantity, δ. This basically means that whatever the performance on the training set, it should probably be pretty close to the corresponding performance once deployed.

Note that this does not say that the in-sample errors (Ein) are any good in an absolute sense. It just says that you should not expect much different after deployment. Thus, good generalization means no surprises after deployment, not necessarily good performance, by any means. There are two main ways to get at this: cross-validation and probability inequalities. For cross-validation, there are two entangled issues: the complexity of the hypothesis set and the probability of the data. It is possible to separate these two by deriving a separate notion of complexity free from any particular data probability. *VC Dimension*. First, there is a need to quantify model complexity. Let A be a class of sets and F = {x1, x2,...,xn}, a set of n data points. Then, define

$$NA(F) = \#\{F \cap A : A \in A\}$$

This counts the number of subsets of F that can be extracted by the sets of A. The number of items in the set (i.e., cardinality) is noted by the # symbol. For example, suppose F = {1} and A = {(x $\leq$ a)}. In other words, A consists of all intervals closed on the right and parameterized by a. In this case, you have NA(F) =1 because all elements can be extracted from F using A.

The shatter coefficient is defined as,

$$s(A,n) = \max_{F \in Fn} N_A(F)$$

where F consists of all finite sets of size n. Note that this sweeps over all finite sets so you don't need to worry about any particular data set of finitely many points. The definition is concerned with A and how its sets can pick off elements from the data set. A set F is shattered by A if it can pick out every element in it. This provides a sense of how the complexity in A consumes data. In the last example, the set of half-closed intervals shattered every singleton set $\{x1\}$.

Now, this leads to the main definition of the Vapnik-Chervonenkis dimension d_{VC} which defined as the largest k for which $s(A,n) = 2^k$, except in the case where $s(A,n) = 2^n$ for which it is defined as infinity. For the example where F $=\{x1\}$, you already saw that A shatters F. How about when F $= \{x1, x2\}$?

Now, there are two points and you have to consider whether all subsets can be extracted by A. In this case, there are four subsets,

$$\{\ \emptyset, \{x1\}, \{x2\}, \{x1, x2\}\ \}$$

Note that $\emptyset$ denotes the empty set. The empty set is easily extracted—pick α so that it is smaller than both x_1 and x_2. Assuming that $x_1 < x_2$, you can get the next set by choosing $x_1 < a < x_2$. The last set is likewise do-able by choosing $x_2 < a$. The problem is that it's not possible to capture the third set, $\{x_2\}$, without capturing x_1 as well. This means that it's not possible to shatter any finite set with n $= 2$ using A. Thus, $d_{VC} = 1$. Here is the climatic result

$$E_{out}(f) \leq E_{in}(f) + \sqrt{\frac{8}{n}}\ ln\ \left(\frac{4((2n)dVC + 1)}{\delta}\right)$$

with probability at least $1-\delta$. This basically says that the expected out-of-sample error can be no worse than the in-sample error plus a penalty due to the complexity of the hypothesis set. The expected in-sample error comes from the training set but the complexity penalty comes from just the hypothesis set, so you have disentangled these two issues. A general result like this, for which you do not worry about the probability of the data, is certain to be pretty generous, but nonetheless, it tells you how the complexity penalty enters into the out-of-sample error. In other words, the bound on $E_{out}(f)$ gets worse for a more complex hypothesis set. Thus, this generalization bound is a useful guideline but not very practical if the plan is to get a good estimate of $E_{out}(f)$.

Conclusion

Now, you've taken a step in the thousand-mile journey, you've read this book. The concepts and technique learned in this book is designed to guide beginners and submerge them into the world of data science. While you learned some complicated programs and techniques, there still room to learn more. There's more to statistics, probability, machine learning, and most of the topics taught in the book. The basics taught here should pique your interest and make you uncomfortable until you've mastered all there is to know about data science.

Python isn't the only programming language that is used for data science; it's just best to learn Python 'first'. You can move on to other programming languages and test your skills there, with the knowledge and skills you've acquired here on python it won't be so difficult master other programming languages.

Machine learning is an entire field on its own, and there are numerous resources available that digs deeper into the subject than what's taught here. The chapter on machine learning in this book will serve as the foundation you need for future learning.

If you're satisfied with the knowledge learned in this book, the next course of action is to *practice, practice, practice!* You already learned how to find and mine data in chapter 9, put it to use. There's data everywhere around you, start analyzing and solving problems. Have fun creating algorithms that have impact in the society. If your intention is to start a career with the skills learned here, participate in competitions to improve yourself. The Internet is full of sites that offer rewards to the winners of the competitions, sometimes employment opportunities.

If you don't succeed or solve the desired problem with the first program you write, don't get discouraged, call it version 1.0 and keep upgrading till you achieve your goal.

"Inspiration is cheap, but rigor is expensive" – let this famous data science quote be your watchword. Good luck.

Resources

Grus, J. (2015). *Data science from scratch: first principles with Python.* First edition. Sebastopol, CA: O'Reilly.

Matthes, E. (2016). Python crash course: A hands-on, project-based introduction to programming.

Johansen A. (2016). *Python: The Ultimate Beginner's Guide!* CreateSpace Independent Publishing Platform.

https://towardsdatascience.com/a-definitive-guide-to-the-world-within-data-science-90300bf6330

https://guide.freecodecamp.org/python

https://medium.com/@rathi.ankit/linear-algebra-for-data-science-a9648b9daee0

https://www.scrapehero.com/tutorial-howu-to-scrape-amazon-product-details-using-python/

https://www.sas.com/en_us/insights/analytics/what-is-a-data-scientist.html

https://beginnersbook.com/2018/01/python-for-loop/

https://sefiks.com/2017/08/07/a-software-engineers-guide-to-becoming-data-scientist/

https://www.python.org/

https://www.geeksforgeeks.org/python-list/

https://www.softwaretestinghelp.com/python/python-data-types/

https://www.w3schools.com

https://www.programiz.com/python-programming

https://www.tutorialspoint.com/python

https://www.analyticsvidhya.com/blog/2017/05/41-questions-on-statisitics-data-scientists-analysts/